855, FILTON AVENUE.

THE
HARLEQUINS

125 Years of Rugby Football

THE HARLEQUINS

125 Years of Rugby Football

PHILIP WARNER

First published in Great Britain by
The Breedon Books Publishing Company Limited
44 Friar Gate, Derby DE1 1DA
1991

ISBN 1 873626 00 2

Printed and bound in Great Britain by Bath Press, Bath and London.
Jacket printed by The Nuffield Press of Cowley, Oxford.

Contents

Early Days 13
Twickenham and After 40
Consolidation 52
The Thirties 62
Rebuilding 78
From the Fifties to the Sixties 106
Into the Depths and Out Again 140
Here and Now......................................170
Tours and Sevens 186
Now and Then 198
Injury Time 208
Extra-time 212
Presidents 234
Secretaries 237
Captains..239
Internationals 240
Subscribers 250

Dedication

To the Harlequins

Introduction by David Brooks
President, Harlequin FC

THE 1991-92 season will see the 125th anniversary of the founding of the Harlequin FC.

The first of many events we shall hold to mark this occasion will be the launching of this up-to-date history of the club which has been written by Philip Warner.

We are fortunate in having a colourful and eventful 125 years of history. This book, which includes many stories of past and present personalities, tells us how the Harlequin style of play began and how it has been maintained through the years.

I am sure you will find it a fascinating story.

David Brook

Foreword
by Peter Winterbottom

CAPTAINING a club is a great honour as it means that you have the approval of the team and the Committee. Being chosen to captain the Harlequins adds an extra dimension, for you know that you have such illustrious predecessors as Adrian Stoop, Wavell Wakefield, Ricky Bartlett, Bob Hiller and many more, and that you have a great tradition of open play behind you.

This could be a weighty burden but, in the event, it proves an asset, for the whole club is dedicated to the idea of lively, attacking football, and all you need to do is try to lead from the front.

My time as captain has been immensely enjoyable in every way. Our aim has been to play good football, win as many matches as we could and enhance the great reputation of the club; when we have done so, it has been because the whole club is one united team. Long may it continue.

Foreword
by Will Carling

SOON after I joined the Harlequins I was appointed to captain England, which gave me plenty to think about. When I played for the Quins I had no such responsibilties as a captain and was therefore able to enjoy the game much more.

The Harlequins have always believed in playing cheerful, light-hearted rugger and making attacks from the most unlikely positions, so that sort of Rugby Football was just what was needed as a relaxation from the international scene.

The Harlequins have never lost sight of the fact that the game is for the enjoyment of fifteen players and all the spectators, whichever side they support. The history of the club shows that adventurous rugger is usually successful, winning both games and friends.

In a recent Cup match we attacked from *behind* our own goal-line and won the game. That is the way Rugby Football should be played and I am particularly glad that the Harlequins have always played that way, in good times and bad, and will continue to do so in the future.

OFFICERS 1991

Early Days

'THEY never miss an opportunity of throwing the ball about with a freedom bordering on recklessness, but they have learnt the art not only of passing, but of taking the ball with safe hands.'

This comment on Harlequin play might have been made yesterday but in fact it was written by a Welshman ninety years ago. The Welsh have always been quick to appreciate creative Rugby Football (and to play it) but do not praise without good reason. Of course, as every Harlequin, and spectator, knows, the hands are not always as safe as they might be and there are times in the strenuously-fought competitions of today when recklessness would mean disaster, but overall the words are as true now as they were then. All Harlequins believe in the open game. Many a newly-joined innocent who has just saved an awkward situation by a timely kick to touch has been crushed by an icy remark from his captain, 'In the Harlequins we don't kick the ball, we pass it'.

Sometimes the Quins have tended to overdo it. In the 1980s there was an enthusiastic spectator in the West Stand at Twickenham who was endowed with a remarkably penetrating voice. On occasions when the Harlequins had been over-elaborate and thus created a disastrous situation, he would call out, 'Oh, you...Quins!' During the slight pause between 'You' and 'Quins', all the other spectators held their breath, wondering whether he was going to use a word which many thought might be more appropriate. Mercifully, he never did.

Every club in the country would dearly love to beat the Harlequins but nobody seems to want anyone else to do it. The Harlequin style of play is accepted as a core element in Rugby Football and all rugger players, whether they acknowledge it or not, like to see the Quins up at the top. This does not prevent some very ambivalent attitutudes. The writer recalls a conversation with a famous Scottish international. 'When I go out to play against the Quins,' he said, 'I hate them intensely, yet when I meet them off the field I find them very easy to get on with.'

Although the Harlequin spirit has remained unchanged over the last 125 years, the club, its organisation, and training, have altered beyond all recognition. Even fifty years ago, Rugby Football was a very casual affair and the Quins were as casual, if not more so, then anyone. Players rarely practised together between matches and a game of squash was regarded as an adequate means of keeping fit.

No longer is it so. Anyone who does not turn up for training sessions, which are usually held up to four times a week, will not be selected to play. Members of teams get to know each other. In past decades players rarely saw each other between matches and might not know each other's names if they did. Today's training sessions often involve players in extensive travelling, although it seems doubtful whether any modern player lives quite as far away from London, and has travelled as far to matches, as some of the old timers occasionally did.

One further point before we plunge into the narrative. Contrary to general belief, the Harlequins are not a snobbish club (although they might have been in the past occasionally). Although there have been many public schoolboys and Oxford and Cambridge blues in their ranks over the years, there have been plenty of players who were proud to describe themselves as classless. Nobody cares about a member's social or educational background. All that matters is that he plays Harlequin-style rugger and puts every ounce into it.

When the Harlequin Football Club began, as the Hampstead FC, in 1866, the game of Rugby Football bore little resemblance to the modern version. Teams were twenty a side, and even this was considered a revolutionary change for, not long before when the game was still in its infancy at Rugby School, the 'sides' had contained a hundred or even more. At that stage the players were divided into forwards, dodgers, and in-quarters. With such huge numbers on the field, the only way of getting near the ball was to kick a path towards it, a process known as 'hacking'. Although hacking was abolished in 1871, the Harlequins team would have 'hacked' for their first five years. In 1860 a Rugby schoolboy had given a vivid description of this murderous type of play; it ended with the words, 'My maxim is to hack the ball on when you see it near you, and when you don't, why then hack the fellow next to you'. However, you were not allowed to hold the person you were hacking.

Hacking was abolished (officially) by the newly-formed Rugby Football Union in 1871, although even in 1991 some players still seem to be unaware of this fact. Referees and touch judges cannot see everything!

The other great difference between then and now was the method of scoring. Originally, points could only be scored by kicks at goal, and kicks at goal could only be taken after a player had crossed his opponents' goal-line and touched the ball down. When this happened, everyone would shout, 'A try, a try', indicating that a member of his team must now be allowed to attempt to kick the ball over the crossbar. Kicks were taken from fifteen yards out and could be charged as soon as the placer put the ball down. After a while, the 'try' became a score in its own right, and three tries were reckoned to equal one goal; today, of course, it is held in much higher esteem than a goal and is therefore worth more points.

The Harlequins were not the first Rugby Football club to be formed, but were fifth equal, sharing that position with Bradford and Liverpool. Blackheath, Richmond, Manchester and Bath were ahead of them. The Quins' first season was 1866-67 and they took the field as Hampstead Football Club, wearing gold and black, with the monogram HFC on their jerseys. The club motto was 'Numquam Dormio' (Never Asleep).

Appropriately, in view of their later light-hearted ventures into cricket, the new club played on the ground which is now used by the Hampstead Cricket Club. However, by 1869, the club was attracting members who had no connection with Hampstead and, as they were no longer able to use the Hampstead ground, they decided to change the club's name.

Rumour has it that everyone liked the monogram so much that the new name had to begin with 'H'. Somebody suggested 'Harlequins'. A Harlequin was a lively, unpredictable, character in Italian comedies and English pantomimes, who wore distinctive multi-coloured clothing. The *Oxford Dictionary* also informs the Harlequins that the word derives from 'Herlequin: the leader of a legendary nocturnal troop of demon horsemen'. One great virtue of the name was that it preserved a light-hearted attitude and prevented anyone getting pompous or too serious; it also meant the Quins didn't 'belong' to any particular location.

Having left Hampstead Cricket Club in 1869, the Quins settled on to a ground at Highbury, called The Old Sluice House. The changing accommodation was a little too primitive, even for the rugged Quins of those days, so after two years they moved to the cricket ground at Tufnell Park. (In the 1950s, when the Quins did not see eye-to-eye with the Rugby Union over the club's use of Twickenham, they gave serious consideration to playing on the Surrey cricket ground at The Oval). Tufnell Park was their home for a mere year and then the Quins were off to Swiss Cottage and changing 'facilities' (as they were called) at a pub called 'The Britannia'. This was not ideal either, so 1873 saw the Harlequins make a giant leap to the other side of London which came down at Putney Heath. Here 'The Green Man' obliged with a changing-room, some hot water, and, no doubt, the means of slaking thirsts.

But not for long. A year later the Quins were at Kensal Green, being hosted by 'The King William IV' ('A good sovereign but a little cracked' they used to say about that monarch), only to move to Hammersmith the following year. Here there was an inn called 'The Queen of England', but both it and the ground seem to have now disappeared under other buildings.

The Harlequins' nomadic existence continued. From Hammersmith they moved to Turnham Green and then to Devonshire Park, Chiswick, before settling on Chiswick Park cricket ground. Here the Quins managed to stay for twelve years and they had hoped that Chiswick would be their permanent home, but it was not to be: the ground was sold in 1897 and the next stopping place was Catford. However, Catford could not retain the Harlequins for long and the club was soon at Wimbledon on a ground whose precise location is not exactly known, although is thought to have been close to the tennis courts.

After two years the Quins were on the move again, this time to Wandsworth Common, where there was actually a pavilion on the ground itself. Perhaps the most remarkable aspect of this saga of constantly changing grounds (which may well be a record) was that the club was increasing in size and reputation all the time. It was, however, nothing to the dramatic expansion which would occur in the next nine years, when Adrian Stoop was creating a revolution in playing style.

On the strength of the reputation that gave the Quins, they were invited to put in a bid to play regularly on the new Rugby Football Union ground at Twickenham. The RFU felt that this would accustom members of the public to making their way to Twickenham, and they would then do the same for international matches. The Quins welcomed the opportunity and it now looked, at long last, as if the club had reached a permanent home, even though only as lease-holders. As it happened, nobody else particularly wanted Twickenham at that time, although subsequently there have been mutterings that the privilege of playing there should have been shared with other clubs.

In fact, Twickenham has been a mixed blessing. The stands are so vast that the normal club attendance looks completely insignificant, and playing in the middle of empty stands is not the most heart-warming experience. Another more serious aspect of the First XV playing at Twickenham has been its effect on club unity. Until the development of the Stoop Ground, where everyone is mixed up together, the First XV and the rest were poles apart. They never practised together, nor could they drink and socialise with the other teams in the bar as other clubs used to do.

However, it should be remembered that the Quins were not absolutely alone in having a First XV which lived in splendid insolation. Certain clubs, such as Leicester, did not even run second teams at all until late this century.

Instead they had about eighteen players who formed what would nowadays be called the first-team squad and, if further reserves were needed, one of the local clubs, or a player from the services or universities, was hastily recruited to plug the gap. Nowadays all clubs seem to have learnt the lesson that a good First XV needs a substantial force of reserves and a 'club' should have a social side.

Twickenham in the early days, and for a quite a long time afterwards, was an ordinary field, on which cattle, sheep or horses grazed when it was not required for matches. Although their presence must have helped the grass to grow, as well as keeping it cropped, the players might not have been over-appreciative of their other contributions. The Rugby Union had bought the field a year earlier, for just under £6,000, and built two small stands which were thought to be adequate for the spectators of international matches. The ground acquired the nickname of 'Billy Williams' Cabbage Patch' because Mr Williams, a Harlequin, had been one of the prime movers in the purchase. But as the Harlequins have now reached Twickenham, we need to retrace our steps and look at the stalwarts who had built up the club sufficiently to make it suitable to play there.

According to our early records (assiduously collected by Nick Cross), the Quins' first *recorded* match was against Clapton at Hackney Down on 16 November 1867. It was described as 'hard contested' and Clapton won by two goals to nil. The Quins lost their next game, against University College, London, the following February, but when they next met Clapton, on 21 March 1868, 'both clubs had strong teams who contested so evenly that at the end of two hours the game was drawn'. This and most of the following reports come from *The Sportsman*, a long defunct paper.

The Sportsman reported a match against City of London School on 4 April 1868: 'Hampstead (*The Quins*) were three men short but after a hard struggle of three hours, neither club had obtained a goal and the match was therefore drawn'. Two hours and three hours: those were the days of real men.

The Harlequins also played St Bartholomew's Hospital, and teams called Parkfield, Mars, the Red Rovers, and the Gipsies in these early days. *The Sportsman* reported: 'During a game against Clapton (*on 16 January 1869*) the Hampstead captain met an accident, breaking one of his fingers by coming into contact with the iron railing. It would be as well if the Clapton men were to play more in the centre of the downs, where there is plenty of room.' During this game, which the Harlequins won, the Quins fielded only ten men against Clapton's eleven. The teams changed ends not once, but twice.

The mainstay of the team in these early days appears to have been E.E.Clarke, who was also the captain. His name first appears in February 1868 and his companions were: Bullen, Headley, Hutchinson, Lipscombe, Nume, Reid, Schooling, Schultze, W.E.Titchener, Tomlinson and Watts. The team was made up to fifteen by three substitutes.

In later matches, Clarke sometimes had two sub captains (officially). Yardley major and Yardley minor also appear. City of London School were frequent opponents in the first few years. Titchener appears to have been a reporter for *The Field* and B.Francis for *The Sportsman*. No doubt they described the games with complete impartiality. Perhaps the Quins should find room for sports reporters among their forwards today.

On 16 October 1869, there was the first glimpse of Harlequin style. Against Red Rovers, at Finchley Road, C.E.Atkinson ran a hundred yards for his touchdown. For the next four matches he was captain, and then Titchener took up that duty again. Clarke was still playing but had long since abandoned the captaincy.

On 30 October 1869, the Quins played (with eleven men) the Blackheath Proprietary School. It really was spelt 'Proprietary', and from its old boys the Blackheath team had originated. At least they managed to put fifteen players in the field, whilst the Quins could only muster eleven.

The Harlequins played their first game against Richmond, at the Old Deer Park, on 27 November 1869. They fielded ten against Richmond's eleven and the game ended in a draw. The following month Titchener was captain, although Atkinson was playing and E.E.Clarke had become E.Ellice-Clarke. In this match, against

Ealing Wanderers played at Finchley Road, W.A.Smith makes his first appearance. Smith was a man of considerable versatility. Not only was he a reliable and competent Harlequin, but he was also a racing cyclist (on penny-farthing bicycles) and a talented concert singer. Later he became secretary and, after that, president.

The Quins' worst performance as regards turnout was against Whitton Park, at Whitton, on 5 February 1870, when the club could muster only eight against their opponents' twelve. The game was lost, but not by much. However, in March, the Quins turned out twelve against St Mary's Hospital's nine and beat them by four goals to nil.

Doubtless there were some sharp words from the captain after these poor turnouts, for from then on the Quins mustered fifteen (usually). However, on 9 February 1870, they played their first seven-a-side game, against Christ's College, Finchley. It was reported in *The Field* for Saturday, 12 February as follows:

This match was played at Finchley on Wednesday last, and resulted in a draw in favour of the college by one touchdown and two rouges. The ball was started shortly after three by the Harlequins, who were, however, soon driven back to their lines, and a touchdown obtained; but the place kick was missed. Half-time being called and ends changed, the Harlequins got better together, and for some time kept the ball in close proximity to the college goal; but Hornsby, by a good run, carried it to neutral ground, where it mostly remained until the end of the game. The field was covered with snow, causing play on both sides to be anything but good; the college more especially were in very bad form. G.F.Henderson and A.Hornsby for their respective sides rendered themselves most conspicuous throughout the game.

It was a drawn game because no goals were scored. A 'rouge' was a touchdown made from under the scrum in what would now be called a pushover try. An ordinary touchdown was made when a player ran over the line with the ball. The word 'rouge' originated with the Eton Field Game which bears some resemblance to Rugby Football.

Wakelam printed a fixture card for the 1870-71 season which, he said, was in a book of Press cuttings. Unfortunately, the original has disappeared. However, when one compares this fixture card with the matches reported in the newspapers of the day, it is obvious that the fixture card is more optimistic than accurate. Eventually the Quins played more matches than appear on the card, but mostly against different opponents. They began that season on 24

September and played such teams as Burlington House and Ravenscourt Park, as well as their old friends, St Bartholomew's Hospital, St Thomas's, St Mary's, and Epsom College: perhaps the Quins had a number of doctors or medical students among their members in those days.

There is no doubt that raising fifteen players was no easy task. In 1871, international games were played between teams of twenty a side (we have pictures of them) but twenty seems beyond the capacity of a club side. Sometimes, however, a latecomer would turn up unnoticed and join in. There was no need to obtain the permission of the referee in those days. An extra man apparently joined in the game against Ealing (on their side) and was not noticed until just before the end. It was described as 'an oversight' by the captain.

But numbers of members were creeping up. By the end of the 1872 season, the Quins held a committee meeting which was attended by thirty, all of whom stayed to dinner.

The Field correspondent is a valuable source of information about this period in the Harlequins' history. One of his better efforts refers to an occasion when Titchener had his jersey torn in the opening minutes and played the game half naked. *The Field* correspondent broke into verse and quoted a mangled version of Alexander Pope's couplet, 'Lo, the poor Indian . . .' as 'Like the poor Injun whose untutored mind/Clothes him in front, but leaves him bare behind'. Doubtless this was what was described as 'creative' writing. Titchener reported for *The Field*, so no doubt he was giving himself a little publicity.

Wasps appeared on the fixture list in March 1872, but the result of what was presumably the Quins' first match against them was not recorded. The Civil Service appears in October 1872, and they had to borrow five Harlequins players. The Quins lost to Cambridge University in November, in a match in which they had fifteen players to the University's sixteen. The Wasps were met again in December 1872, in a drawn match, and the Quins also drew with Richmond, with seventeen a side.

The reports of some of these early matches give the occasional result 'draw in favour'. This meant that no goals had been kicked but one side had secured more touchdowns (or tries or rouges) than the other.

The year 1873 saw the birth of a Second XV, bringing the total number of matches played in that season up to thirty-nine. Oxford University appear in November 1873, but obviously the club's main rivals were Richmond, for the Quins played them with seventeen or (once) eighteen a side.

Cheltenham College, a stronghold of the game, had an old boys' side called the the Old Cheltonians. When the Quins played them in January 1874, both teams had two full-backs, two half-backs and two quarter-backs. October 1874 finds the Harlequins playing the Stock Exchange and defeating them; they could only muster thirteen men to the Quins' fourteen. There was another unusual fixture that month, against the Indian Civil Engineering College at Cooper's Hill. The Quins drew this one but lost to Sandhurst a week later. Flamingoes were still frequent opponents but one of these games, played in Battersea Park, was terminated fifteen minutes early by the Harlequins because the spectators insisted on joining in. Football hooligans are not a twentieth-century invention.

Streatham and the Royal Naval College at Greenwich were also on the club's list. Walthamstow were beaten in January 1876, in a game that had to be abandoned through darkness; late kick-offs were a problem which was to be expected when grounds were remote and difficult to find.

An interesting fixture, originally arranged for December 1876 but which was postponed and played the following March, was against the German Gymnastic Society, at Haverstock Hill, Hampstead. Nobody appears to know whether these were Germans in Britain, or merely British who practised the German style of gymnastics. It seems likely that it was the latter. However, in later years, Germany often appeared on the Quins' fixture list. Up until the present day (1991), the German national XV, although worthy of the club's First XV fixture list, has so far failed to reach the height of dedication and performance reached by other European countries, such as France, Italy and Romania. Doubtless its turn will come.

The year 1876 was the first in which the number of players in a team was officially reduced to fifteen. But there was still some way to go before the game began to take the shape its modern counterpart.

The Harlequins' relationship with Wasps seems to have been very friendly. The Quins borrowed their ground when their own was under repair for the cricket season.

In November 1878, London Scottish appear on the fixture list, in a drawn game, and in 1881 the Quins lost their first game against the Royal Military Academy at Woolwich. In that same year, the Quins lost by a try to a goal to the famous Marlborough Nomads.

Harlequin FC, 1880-81, the earliest known photograph. Back row (left to right); F.G.C.Burnand, C.Job, A.Claremont, C.E.Grasserman, A.T.Waley, J.C.Howe, A.E.Stoddart. Middle row: H.Watts, E.H.Coles, A.Tillyer (captain), C.E.Macrae, H.L.Stoddart, L.Waver. Front row: E.Kell, F.S.Watts, R.W.Burnand.

The match against Cardiff at Cardiff on 1 April 1882 was a draw, but attracted 1,500 spectators. It was the first time a metropolitan team had appeared in Wales. In December 1882 the Quins played ther first game against the Twickenham club and beat them by four goals and five tries to nil. In February 1883, the Quins again drew with Cardiff, but this time at home. A month later they lost to them by a goal, this time at Turnham Green.

In October 1883, the Harlequins played Newport for the first time, and lost by four tries to nil. The Quins arrived two players short and had to borrow two from Cardiff to make up their numbers. The next day they played Cardiff and drew with them. No doubt the Cardiff team had arrived at Newport to get a look at their prospective opponents, but can hardly have expected to give them a helping hand.

In 1883, the Quins were at Chiswick Park and obviously firmly established. A note was sent to members specially requesting that they should always play in club colours; the mind boggles at the thought of half the team being dressed as Harlequins and the remainder in whatever happened to be handy and reasonably clean. In these days of washing machines and powerful detergents it may be overlooked that the mudstained clothes of our forebears were washed with inadequate soap and scrubbed (almost) clean by industrious washerwomen.

W.R.M.Leake, then a master at Dulwich, was the Quins' first international, playing half-back against Scotland, Ireland and Wales in 1891. Leake was not only an inspiration to the club but also a very good channel for promising recruits. Over the years the Harlequins have had good reason to be grateful to members who were schoolmasters, who encouraged promising players to join the club.

This useful source of young talent was later supplemented by the practice of the Quins' 'A' team playing against the leading rugger schools. Before taking the field, the 'A' team were instructed that, even if their young opponents, and a partisan referee, bent the rules, there must be absolutely no obvious resentment, as the aim was to show what nice chaps the Quins were and how desirable it would be to join the club. It was rumoured that certain keen secretaries carried a few Harlequin ties in their pockets which were then presented to particularly promising players, who became members on the spot. The same story was recounted about other clubs but is thought to be apocryphal.

A.B.Cipriani, in company with W.A.Smith, played for the First XV for fifteen consecutive seasons, a feat which remains unmatched. Other stalwarts of those early days were A.E.Stoddart and F.W.Burnand.

In 1886 the Quins had a full fixture card. The First XV is shown as playing Blackheath, London Scottish, Richmond, Oxford, Cambridge, Sandhurst, Woolwich, Moseley (although the match was scratched) and Birkenhead Park, who defeated the Quins. Of the school fixtures, Dulwich College alone survived, but the Quins played three old boys' sides: Cheltonians (Cheltenham), Old Rugbeians (of whom a number were also playing for the Harlequins) and Marlborough Nomads. The last was a formidable team which had been pioneers of the game but which failed to survive. In all there were twenty-five First XV fixtures and twenty-three Second XV games.

The following year the Quins became even more venturesome, travelling to Birkenhead Park and Weston-super-Mare. That year also saw the appearance of 'Billy' Williams, whom we mentioned in connection with Twickenham, and Rowland Hill. Billy Williams, although never an international, was a leading figure in the club for many years; he was also an outstanding cricketer and was still playing in 1939. Rowland Hill's services to the game are commemorated by the Rowland Hill Gate on the south-west entrance to Twickenham.

The year 1888 had seen the first appearance of C.M.Wells, who subsequently played for England, five times against Scotland and twice against Wales but never against Ireland. A product of Dulwich and Cambridge, he won blues at both Rugby Football and cricket. For his first blue he played full-back, but later moved up to half. On going down from Cambridge he became an Assistant Master at Eton. Playing during the holidays presented no problem but in term time, with lessons taking place on Saturday mornings,

Harlequin FC, 1885-6. W.R.M.Leake is second from right in the back row. F.W.Burnand is now the captain. All are still wearing knickerbockers and some of the jerseys look home-made.

he had to rush off after school, miss lunch, change in the guard's van of the train and run to Chiswick Park just in time for the kick-off. Many later Harlequins will no doubt recall similar experiences when work or other commitments made their arrival on the ground a matter of split-second timing. Fellow passengers view the emergence of a multi-coloured figure from the guard's van with surprise bordering on alarm.

Wells spoke highly of the even ground at Chiswick Park, where the grass was short, but described the accommodation in the pavilion as 'primitive', not without cause: it consisted of four or five small basins of cold water for the whole XV to share. Later, the unprecedented luxury of a hip bath with hot water was introduced. However, he once commented: 'I don't think players were so

particular in those days.' If these were the washing facilities after the club had been in existence for twenty-two years, one blenches at what they must have been like in the earlier days. Changing accommodation has, of course, improved miraculously in recent years, but there are plenty of present-day members who can recall communal baths which were full of water which was either scaldingly hot or lukewarm and in which the effect was often to distribute the mud more evenly rather than to remove it.

In Wells' day, both half-backs stood close to the scrum and worked independently to the three-quarters. He records that, when playing for the Harlequins, but only then, he would sometimes tell his fellow half to stand close to the scrum while he stood further back. This originated the term 'stand-off half' and also the expression 'inside' half and 'outside' half. When Adrian Stoop came into the game a few years later, he immediately fastened on to the tactical possibilities of a stand-off half and created a revolutionary style of half-back play to go with it.

Wells also records that, although the Harlequins were by no means the strongest side in the country, they were not easy to beat for they had a disconcerting (to their opponents) habit of suddenly making an unorthodox move which frequently produced a winning score. He also noted that when on tour, the Harlequins were 'a very steady lot of fellows compared with other clubs', and this moderation often brought success. By 'steady' he presumably meant 'sober and abstemious'. He also spoke of upholding the tradition of the Harlequins, although whether this meant to remain 'steady' on tour seems open to debate. However, it is significant that there was already a Harlequin 'tradition' before the Stoop era.

Wells described a Christmas tour on which the Harlequins beat Rugby, drew with Coventry and beat Leicester. He thought the last game was 'unforgettable'. As an experiment the ground had been covered with sand, rather than straw, to protect it against frost. In the event there was no frost but instead a continuous downpour of rain. When the match was played, the 'turf' looked like a sea-shore with large pools of water dotted here and there. Fortunately for the Harlequins, they were still playing in knickerbockers, or they might have left most of the skin off their knees on the ground. As it was, many of them abandoned their clothing after the game as being too sodden and sandy to take away.

Not least of the Harlequins' achievements at this time was the fact that the club was solvent.

In the 1890-91 season, the Quins ran First, Second and Third

The Harlequins in 1895. Now they are in (long) shorts but individual stockings. Back row (left to right): R.W.Hunt, H.S.Clarke, H.S.P.Hindley, J.N.Hill, J.D.Whittaker, J.L.Phillips, H.P.Surtees. Middle row: A.B.Cipriani, J.R.Pauk, S.B.Beech, H.R.Wood, C.M.Wells. Front row: W.J.Susmann, P.S.Saward, C.Wells.

XVs, but this was eclipsed the following year when an additional team, labelled 'A', appeared between the First and Second XVs. However, the strain of running four XVs was apparently too demanding and in 1892 the number fell back to three, although the 'A' still appeared uneasily poised between the First and Second. That year there were 263 members, but no doubt most of them must have retired from playing.

In 1893, Dublin Wanderers made their first appearance at Chiswick Park. Overall this was a successful season. One of the victories was over London Welsh with a score of 41-0.

In 1894 a list of rules appeared. This gave the subscription as 10s 6d (53p) and listed the categories of members as active, honorary and life. The latter paid five guineas (£5.25) for the privilege. Rule 20 was approximately equal to our present Rule XX, which gives favourable terms to 'students', which is a fairly broad definition.

An early action picture, possibly from the 1890s. Note the shape of the ball and the players' lace-up collars and buckle belts, although they are all now wearing shorts.

However, there was also a Rule 14 which struck a sterner note by imposing a fine on any member, the sum of 2s 6d (13p), if he failed to play after having promised to do so.

The 1895-96 season was another good campaign; three teams playing a combined total of seventy-four games, of which forty-six were won, twenty-one lost and seven drawn. Unfortunately the Quins did not attract many paying spectators for these achievements and had to dig into their reserves to pay their annual rent of £20 to Chiswick Park.

The following year the Quins produced a fourth team once more, although this time they called it a 'B' side. The club was now temporarily at Catford, having lost their excellent Chiswick Park ground through no fault of their own. However, the 'B' lasted two years only and 1898 was apparently a year in which the club struggled to exist at all.

The following two years were not much better. By 1900 it seemed as if the Harlequin Football Club might be wound up, but when this crisis had passed, owing to a whip-round by members, the

Harlequins took on a new lease of life. It was undoubtedly the darkest hour before the dawn, for in the following year the Quins entered on the Stoop era and a greatly strengthened fixture list.

In 1901 the Harlequins staged their first fixture with the Racing Club de France, which was the forerunner of several. As it was a home match, the Quins were asked for a substantial guarantee, eventually settled at £30. Although the French had been playing Rugby Football for at least twenty years, they had not yet made enough progress to put out an international team. That day would come, with a vengeance.

The years 1899-1902 were, of course, the period of the South African War, and this undoubtedly sapped the Harlequins' playing strength, for large numbers would have volunteered for military service. However, by 1902, when they had settled at Wandsworth Common, the Quins found themselves with a nucleus of highly promising youngsters.

They included R.C.Hayward, A.C.T.Vessey, D.Linton, V.H.Cartwright, who would later be capped fourteen times for England; C.E.L.Hammond, who would secure eight caps; and a half-back who had been spotted when the 'A' side visited Rugby School. His name was Adrian Stoop, who was up at Oxford but not yet a blue, so he could play for the Quins. Genius though he was, it took him seven years to amass his total of fifteen England caps, for he was unlucky with injury. In those days a player was not able to obtain more than three or four international caps in a season; nowadays, of course, with the arrival of touring sides and our own visits overseas, he can double that number.

The year 1902 saw measures of financial prudence. The Racing Club de France fixture disappears temporarily; it was obviously a costly item, whether the Quins played them here or in Paris, and the club also discontinued the system of admitting Life Members by payment. As every secretary soon learns, lump sums payments are a pleasant boost to finances when they arrive but a steady flow of annual subscriptions, which can be increased in amount, provide a more satisfactory income.

In 1902, captain Philip Foster, writing under the name of 'Dux', produced a book entitled *Rugby Football,* in which he has much to say of the Harlequins. As we have no detailed records of the period 1887-1905, although we know the end of the century was an unhappy period, his book, which contains the records from 1896-1902, is invaluable. Fortunately a copy fell into the hands of G.E.Loader (*see later*).

In the 1898-99 season, the Quins won four matches out of twenty-three; in 1889-1900 they won six out of twenty-one; and in 1900-1901, six out of twenty-three. However, in 1901-02 the Quins bounced back and won eleven out of twenty-three.

Foster wrote:

There is not a follower of Rugby Union Football in the neighbourhood of London who will not admit that the Harlequins are amongst the most sportsmanlike of clubs. Unfortunately, for some few years past they have fallen upon evil times. Last season's play, however, was more encouraging. Starting badly, they improved considerably until the middle of November, when they again fell away. I venture to think that when they succeed in winning a match there is no more popular victory. Such popularity is never gained without cause. The lines upon which the Harlequins club was originally promoted, and on which it is still conducted, must very properly appeal to all people whose moral vision, as it were, is not perverted. Essentially amateur, in spirit as well as in fact, is the definition which some years ago I heard applied to this famous old club, and it will generally be admitted that such a definition is well merited. The Harlequins club has had many difficulties with which to contend since its formation. At the risk of disturbing a sleeping dog, so to speak, I cannot but call attention to the fact that in the past more than one player, whose reputation afterwards became world-wide, was content to use the Harlequins' Football Club as a stepping-stone to higher things, higher things, that is to say, as far as his own individual prospects were concerned. There have, I say, been several instances of such defection, and it is therefore all the more pleasant to be able to direct one's attention to an instance of the opposite order of things. It is almost unnecessary for me to say that I allude to Mr Cyril Wells. Certainly he will go down to history as one of the greatest of half-backs; but if the truth must be told, his claims were not always fully appreciated whilst he was a member of the active list, and there is much difference of opinion even at the present time concerning him. Some nine years ago, it will be remembered, the South of England administered a very severe defeat indeed to the North of England. So brilliantly, too, did the winning side play as a whole that, with one single exception, they were all immediately chosen to represent England in the next International match. Queerly enough, that exception was Mr Cyril Wells, who, perhaps if a combination of brains, hand, foot and eye be taken into consideration, was the most brilliant

Harlequin FC, 1902-03. W.A.Smith (president) is in the rear row with cap and beard. C.E.L.Hammond is the captain. A.D.Stoop is seated on the ground, centre front.

individual player of them all. Of course it was contended that he lacked the power to defend. At this time of day it is quite useless to plead on behalf of any man against whom such a charge is preferred. Therefore, without instituting an unprofitable discussion, it may be permitted to me to suggest that Mr Cyril Wells was in the habit of putting his side in the position to attack about three times as often as any other half-back in the four kingdoms. In one particular trick or habit, I doubt if he has ever had an equal. Whether the ball was wet or dry, he had mastered the knack of gathering it, either when it was stationary or in motion, when travelling at a fair rate of speed. I have alluded to Mr Wells's brain, and I should contend that he was worth his place in any side for his generalship alone, quite apart from his proficiency in those clever tactics which are the natural outcome of clever generalship. One other point may be noted, too, in connection with this famous player. Whilst in residence at Cambridge he played at one time or another in every position behind the scrummage. The Harlequins club is the poorer by his retirement after many years of good service, and one looks hopefully forward to the time when they will possess more players of *his stamp. Should they succeed in finding such, the tide of fortune will doubtless at once turn in their favour.*

And, of course, they did, beginning with Adrian Stoop.

Foster, incidentally, was not a Harlequin! So the Quins can print all those kind words he said about their being 'the most sportsmanlike of clubs', give and take a few modest blushes.

In 1903, the Honours cap was introduced. This cap has rarely been awarded and Adrian Stoop said it was rated more highly than an international cap. Club caps are awarded for exceptional service to the club as a player or administrator. Today they entitle the holder to wear a tie with narrower stripes than the standard one; the caps have now become too expensive to produce!

The year 1903 also saw the arrival of the formidable H.E. 'Holly' Ward, whose brother 'Roc' was already a member. Holly was a member of the club for forty-five years and for the last thirty-eight was honorary treasurer. He was a man of great charm and courtesy but stood absolutely no nonsense, either on the field or off it. His style of play was described as 'robust' and it is recorded that once when playing against Northampton he had a personal battle with a notorious forward on the other side. According to Wakelam: 'The referee perhaps was not quite up to it all, and tempers were becoming a little frayed. After one particularly fierce maul, however, the said Northampton forward, on emerging, was heard to remark, "All right, Mr Ward, I give you best," the game thenceforward resuming a more even tenor.' One notes the pleasant old world courtesy of addressing a man as 'Mister' immediately after trying to tear off his genitals.

In 1906 came the establishment of the first of the Harlequins' affiliated clubs from overseas. From South Africa had come an application for permission to form a club there bearing the name of Harlequin FC. It was a sign that the Quins' style of play had attracted attention in that great Rugby-playing country and the Quins were glad to accede to the request. Later there would be other affiliated overseas clubs which the Quins should also regard with justifiable pride.

Although Adrian Stoop had been a member since the beginning of the century, his influence was not fully felt until the 1905-06 season. It is interesting to ponder the fact that Adrian had originally intended to join Blackheath, but had been persuaded by an old schoolmate (Cartwright) to throw in his lot with the Harlequins. Where would the Quins have been without Adrian? It is really impossible to give an adequate description of what he did for the club. Not only was he a great player, but he was also a very

Adrian Stoop in his playing days.

sympathetic and helpful person to those less gifted than himself. With it went a remarkable eye for budding talent.

Unfortunately in his later years he became slightly eccentric and obsessive, which diminished the esteem in which he was held generally, and some of the later captains found him interfering more than they liked; however, this should not be allowed to diminish his legendary stature and his great influence on the game. There have possibly been better stand-off halves but never any so creative. One of his first moves was to choose his scrum-half, H.J.H.Sibree, and soon he had J.G.G.Birkett as a centre three-quarter and D.Lambert as a wing. None of these were ready-made stars: Birkett had joined the club as a half-back and was very disconcerted to find that Adrian had earmarked him as a three-quarter; Lambert had been a soccer player in the Eastbourne College First XI, but become a forward in the XV when they changed over to rugger in 1900. He joined the Quins and became a forward in the 'A' XV. His selection for the Firsts was somewhat unorthodox. In a trial game that season, Adrian Stoop was racing for the line with all the confidence which his recently acquired international status had given him. However, just as he was about to score, he was hurled into touch by what appeared to be a human cannon-ball. Adrian's version was: 'When I recovered I asked, "What the hell was that?" The answer being, "Oh that was Lambert who plays forward for the 'A' ". I said, "Well now he plays wing three-quarter for the First!" '

Lambert was subsequently capped seven times. He scored innumerable tries for the Harlequins, was a superb place-kicker, and tackled, as Adrian Stoop had noticed, like a charging bull. He was a large, genial man who had a long deceptive stride; in consequence many a player who tried to mark him totally miscalculated his speed and was left far behind.

Birkett soon forgot he was a frustrated half-back and went on to win twenty-one England caps.

Stoop, who had a naturalised Dutch father and a mother who was half Scottish and half Irish, was born on 27 March 1883 and died on 27 November 1957. He had begun his education at Dover College, then went on to Rugby and finished at University College, Oxford. Although he did not get a blue in his first year, he won three subsequently. During World War One he served in the Queen's Regiment in Mesopotamia, was wounded and was awarded a Military Cross. He played his last game for the Harlequins at the age of 55, in 1938 against Eastbourne (then a First XV fixture).

Ken Chapman, G.J.Dean, and J.Mycock were in the same team, which lost narrowly.

He was a stickler for physical fitness and attention to detail. The author recalls an occasion after a game at Twickenham on which Adrian harangued the players on the need for the highest standard of mental and physical well-being. He stated firmly that everyone should drink a minimum of four pints of water a day, irrespective of what else was drunk. A few of the more impressionable listeners took this advice seriously. No doubt it was very cleansing but it was too boring and uncomfortable a process to last long, for the water seemed to run out almost as quickly as it went in.

Indulgent parents enabled him to transform his home at Hartley Wintney into a sort of hospitable training camp, and in later years he also managed to secure the use of the enormous playing field at Sandhurst for that purpose on Sunday mornings. Clothing, particularly boots, were in the earlier stages of their development and Adrian was always on the look-out for improved versions.

He was, perhaps, fortunate that in his day he had a pack of massive forwards in front of him and was therefore provided with a plentiful supply of ball. The hooker was 'Roc' Ward, who was said to be so bulky that he virtually constituted an entire front row on his own. Ironically, he was at first rejected on medical grounds for military service in World War One but passed at a later attempt and was killed while leading a tank attack.

Then, as now, a strong pack of forwards was an essential for any successful team. Until the Stoop era, the team had consisted of ten forwards, two quarter-backs, one half-back, and two full-backs. The forwards often employed a manoeuvre which has never lost favour, although its modern version takes a slightly different form. The principle was to form a wedge with the ball at the apex, two men behind it, three more behind them, with arms locked together, and four at the rear. The spare man would push inwards on whatever side seemed most in need of his services. If checked, the 'wedge' would then heel the ball to the quarter-backs.

V.H. 'Harry' Cartwright captained the club in 1905, 1906 and 1907: he played for England fourteen times. He was very fast and a devastating tackler. In those days, and until recently, a scrum which had obtained possession could 'wheel' by swinging round and taking the ball full circle. Cartwright was apparently an expert at beginning a wheel, which, once begun, was very difficult for its opponents to stop: the only method was to fall in front of the advancing forwards and grab the ball which, by that time, was probably being dribbled quite fast; courage was the essence.

Another notable of this era was Edmund Fearenside, who was one of those gifted players who can play successfully in virtually any position. As a hooker he was so quick that spectators assumed he must be striking before the ball was properly in the scrum, and made their view known to the referee who knew, however, that Fearenside was striking legally. He was a contemporary of W.B. Grandage, a greatly esteemed doctor. Like certain other medical men, he preferred an offensive to a defensive role in wartime and commanded an artillery brigade in World War One, during which he was killed.

Nevertheless it was the creative, tactical thinking of Adrian Stoop which brought the Harlequins success in the pre-World War One period rather than the special skills of any individuals. Stoop believed that attacks should be launched from every position, not merely when the attackers were close to the defenders' line. In fact, he pointed out that attacks from near one's own line were more likely to be successful, as the opposing side would be spread widely. But to make sure that desperate attack from one's own 'twenty-five' (now twenty-two metres) line did not turn into diaster, accurate and skilful passing was vital. A pass, according to Adrian, should not be made by propelling the ball with the arms, but by swinging the whole upper body from the waist: the arms would merely guide the ball. He used to advise *all* players, whatever their position on the field, to practise passing by holding the corner of a cushion between their front teeth (if they were lucky enough still to have them). The cushion could then be swung (to either side) by twisting the body. This produced an elegant and effective form of passing. Stoop also insisted that passes should be given and received when the players were running flat out. 'Take your pass when you are running at full speed, and then accelerate.' This classic form of passing did not, of course, preclude the short lobbed pass or 'backhander', when the occasion demanded, but as a principle it was an essential ingredient of Harlequin success.

Stoop's creative play was rewarded not only by successes on the field but also by larger attendances, both home and away. He was not, however, generally credited as having developed his ideas by himself, although he had. Instead, some of his ploys were traced to similar developments in New Zealand, where the game had been played since 1870. New Zealand has never been short of creative Rugby footballers but to attribute Stoop's ideas to them is absurd. A more credible possibility is that he acquired some good ideas from Wales, where players are never more dangerous than when forced back almost on to their own line.

Although much less well known, Adrian had a brother F.M. 'Tim' Stoop, who was a formidable three-quarter. He was taller and heavier than his illustrious brother and was capped for England four times; it was said that a tackle by Tim Stoop was something that most players would hope to avoid.

The other star of that period, and one who would probably have been outstanding at any other time too, was R.W.Poulton, who later became R.W.Poulton-Palmer, as he was heir to his uncle the Rt Hon G.W.Palmer MP, although he never lived to succeed to the estate. His father was a Professor of Zoology at Oxford and 'Ronnie' Poulton had shown his flair for the game when still at Rugby School; he had been in the First XV from the age of sixteen, and three years later he was the mainstay of a team which scored 250 points to 59.

He played his first game for the Harlequins when still a schoolboy but, like Adrian Stoop, did not get a blue in his first year at Oxford. Poulton-Palmer's genius seemed to some of the more conservative element in the game (who did not include Adrian Stoop) too good to be true. It was felt that he was unpredictable (which he was) and that his tackling might be suspect, although it was not. In his very first game for the Quins he had shown what form his unpredictablity could take. He had begun an attacking move from *behind* his own line, and the result had been a try (scored by Lambert) between the opposition posts.

His most memorable try was scored against the hitherto unbeaten Springboks at Twickenham in 1913. The England team had been driven back almost to its own line when the 40,000 spectators suddenly erupted with the cry, 'Poulton's through'. Indeed he was. He had slipped through his exasperated opponents and hared up the entire length of the field to score. Only one person at Twickenham, apart from himself, knew how he had spent the evening before the game. He had always been a strong supporter of the Rugby School Club which ran an establishment at Notting Hill. On calling at the club the evening before the match, he had been told that one of the boys was dying but would like to see him. Without hesitation Poulton-Palmer went to the boy's home and sat by his bed for several hours before he died. The story comes from the manager of the club at the time, the Revd C.S.Donald.

Not surprisingly, Poulton-Palmer was greatly liked by the staff at the Huntley & Palmer biscuit works in Reading, where he worked, and was held in similar esteem in the Royal Berkshire Regiment which he joined in 1914. He was killed by a German sniper on 5 May 1915 at Ploegsteert, Belgium. Modest and unassuming to the point of shyness, Poulton-Palmer was always ready to help others and was an outstanding leader. As might be expected, he was also an excellent hockey player and cricketer. W.J.A.Davies, himself a legendary fly-half and all-games player, said of him: 'For four years preceding the war no personality more completely dominated the rugger world than Ronald Poulton. He was my ideal captain. His extraordinary, deceptive run and swerve made him a most difficult man to tackle. He possessed abnormal football sense and was always there to carry on a movement!'

On and off the field, Ronnie Poulton-Palmer was a man whom the Harlequins are proud to have had as a member. From the early days the Quins had shown a good club spirit in the way in which they supported each other.

They had also taken it for granted that they would often give a helping hand to others less gifted or fortunate than themselves, perhaps by doing a little coaching and, long before the creation of the welfare state, giving up time to work in boys' clubs and do relief work in very poor areas. These attitudes were not unique to Harlequins: plenty of other clubs thought in much the same way.

The 1907-08 season was memorable in many ways. It began with a 42-0 victory over Richmond and continued with a 49-8 victory over Bath. The Quins beat the Racing Club de France 8-0, at Bagatelle (the town, not the game of that name).

At this time the Quins were experimenting with the New Zealand idea of having two fly-halves, one being called a five-eighth. This, of course, meant having three three-quarters instead of four and, as one was Kenneth Powell, an Olympic hurdler, there was no lack of speed among the backs. Unfortunately, Adrian Stoop broke his collarbone in a game against the United Services. For a while this set back both his international career and the smooth running of the club, but he recovered and the Harlequins notched up an 11-0 victory against Blackheath. Although the Quins had been playing Blackheath since 1881, this was only the second time they had beaten them. 'The Club', as they were called (and sometimes still are) were one of the earliest clubs in the country and had had a formidable number of distinguished players. Nevertheless, the Quins beat them twice more that season in games that could be described as 'hard-fought'.

Administratively, the Harlequin FC seemed to be getting on to a sure footing, although they were still nomads as far as grounds were concerned (the Quins were now playing at Wandsworth Common). Finances, though, were now considered sound enough to merit ther club making its first investment. This was £50-worth of 3 per cent India stock. The Quins also developed the social side by having monthly dinners at Simpsons in the Strand. Right up until World War Two, it was possible to have a plate of Simpsons' renowned saddle of mutton (vegetables, of course, included) for three shillings. It is difficult to know how Simpsons ever made a profit, if they did, for their waiters used to carve slices of roast mutton (their speciality) or beef until asked to stop, and Harlequins had always had large appetites. Simpsons still serve excellent saddle of mutton but the quantities and the price have needed to be modified for today's economic realities.

The 1908-09 season looked like being a disaster when both Adrian Stoop and Birkett broke their collarbones playing in a game against the London Scottish, which, nevertheless, was won with thirteen men. This was Stoop's second break in two years.

At the end of the season the Quins took a team to Frankfurt and beat the newly-organised German national XV. After the game there was a social supper, timed for 6pm. Unfortunately, owing to someone's error, the Quins did not arrive till 6.40 and were greeted by resentful silence. The president of the German club, who appears to have had a sense of humour, let the Harlequins sit down and then announced that he and his committee had decided that one of our team should be penalised for this lapse of manners by being made to drink ten glasses of beer. On hearing this, C.E.L. 'Curly' Hammond promptly knocked back six glasses and then, standing on his chair, polished off the remaining four. He then exclaimed: "Now bring me something to drink. I'm thirsty." The Germans, greatly impressed (and pleased), elected him 'Beer king of all Germany'.

That season saw the Harlequins make one of their highest scores so far in beating Surbiton 74-3. They also played the Old Merchistonians (Merchiston Castle School, Edinburgh) who, presumably, were on tour. The Quins played other Old Boys' clubs such as the Old Leysians (Leys School, Cambridge), Old Alleynians (Dulwich College) and Old Merchant Taylors, who had the formidable J.E.Raphael, a three-quarter who played nine times for England.

In one of their last games at Wandsworth Common, the Quins were due to play Coventry but the game was cancelled.

Twickenham
and After

THE Harlequins' first game at Twickenham was against Richmond and took place on 2 October 1909. Modern players will note that although some things have changed, others certainly have not. For one thing, the grass was over-long, just as it is nowadays at the start of the season (in order to preserve the turf as long as possible); for another it was soaking wet. Rain had poured down almost continuously for several days. The third enduring fact about this game was that it was a hard-fought 'local derby'.

Whatever the records of the two clubs may be against other teams, the two annual fixtures are something special and unpredictable. This one ended in a victory for Harlequins by 14 points to 10. Two thousand people watched, and that is about the size of an average crowd today. Richmond seemed to have the edge in the forwards, but the Quins, with the two Stoops, Birkett, Poulton-Palmer and Lambert, had the better backs. Two other notables were G.R.Maxwell-Dove, the full-back, and G.V.Carey in the front row of the scrum.

Maxwell-Dove, who was another product of the Quins' 'nursery' at Rugby, lived in Cumberland but was happy to make what must have been very long and tedious journeys. He appears to have been the holder of the record for distance travelled by a player, although J.G.Willcox, the international full-back of the 1960s, travelled from Preston, Lancashire (where he was stationed with the Army) for two years to play for the Wanderers.

G.V.Carey, a lively, tough forward, was a product of Eastbourne College, to which he later returned as headmaster. George Carey was a brilliant classical scholar who rose to the rank of Lieutenant-Colonel in World War One (Rifle Brigade), and then became a Squadron-Leader in the RAF in the Second. He wrote a very witty little book on punctuation entitled *Mind the Stop*. Carey had the distinction of kicking-off in the Quins' first game at Twickenham.

The team which played the first match at Twickenham in 1909. Standing at left is S.R.Maxwell-Dove. W.A.Smith (president) is seated in the centre. On his right is A.D.Stoop. Extreme right (seated) is R.W.Poulton Palmer.

Very appropriately, the club's first try at Twickenham was scored by Birkett. John Birkett's father, R.H.Birkett, had played in the first international between England and Scotland, back in 1871, and also scored the first-ever try scored for England. R.H.Birkett subsequently played for England four more times at Rugby Football, but also became an international at soccer. John Birkett, who was a product of Haileybury, arrived in the club under the impression that he was a scrum-half, but this view was quickly corrected and he was converted into a three-quarter. His uncle was also an international rugger player; his son played for the club in the Thirties.

An interesting convention dating from the Harlequins' appearance at Twickenham was that any member was allowed to introduce two ladies as spectators free of charge. Whether this meant that the ladies thought there was safety in numbers, or whether no self-respecting Harlequin could content himself with one female partner at a time, is not clear. In recent years the 'two ladies' have become one 'guest'. Nowadays, of course, ladies may be full members of the club and introduce their own guests. This is not merely because this change is in accordance with modern thinking, but also recognises the fact that throughout the club's history, wives, sisters and girl friends have given hours of their time to boring, routine tasks such as serving in bars and tea rooms and being genuinely supportive.

Playing at Twickenham seems to have been heady medicine, for the Quins contrived to win most of their matches during the 1909-10 season, some by substantial margins: 43-0 over London Scottish, 23-3 Bedford, 57-0 Rosslyn Park, 22-3 Blackheath, 30-3 Richmond, 56-0 Marlborough Nomads. The final tally was eighteen wins, four losses and one draw, giving the Harlequins a total of 550 points to 147.

With this success story went a similar one financially. On the strength of it the Quins began to pay the travelling expenses of players in the 'A' team, which performed a useful purpose in

maintaining the club's links with schools. In 1912, H.E.Gardiner was appointed auditor and this represented another dynastic connection with the club. Hubert and his brother, Alfred, played for the club for a long period: Dennys Gardiner, Hubert's son, subsequently was first a player and later treasurer for fifteen seasons, then auditor till 1983.

We have already mentioned the 'wedge' tactics which had proved very popular and successful. However, in 1911 the Rugby Union

Harlequin FC, 1913-14. Back row (left to right): S.H.Lambert, A.C.Palmer, R.W.Ling, J.B.Mudge, K.N.Carnduff, R.M.Gotch, A.H.Hudson, D.O'H.Tripp. Front row: D.Lambert, R.W.Poulton-Palmer, J.G.G.Birkett, A.D.Stoop (captain), R.O.C.Ward, H.J.Sibree, A.F.Q.Perkins. Front row: H.B.T.Wakelam, G.M.Chapman.

decided that from thenceforward it would be illegal to pick up the ball in the scrum and hold it. There was some dismay at this change, as the previous rule had helped to anchor forwards in the pack and prevented them from hanging around the back of the scrum on the look-out for any opportunities, and bending the offside rule. The predatory wing-forward became the blight of open rugger in the Thirties. Eventually his marauding activities were curbed by legislation. Even today, though, free-ranging flankers have to be drawn back into the scrum by tactical ploys.

Swansea appeared at Twickenham in April 1911, in a match drawn 5-5. In the autumn of that year, the Quins seem to have hammered some of their more illustrious opponents: Northampton 32-0, Lansdowne 27-0, Guy's Hospital 35-12, Rosslyn Park 19-0, before losing, surprisingly, to O.M.T.s 0-16, although the Quins took revenge later in a 5-0 win. The 'Old Blues', not, as might be thought, ageing Oxford and Cambridge players, but former pupils of Christ's Hospital, were regularly in the fixtures.

H.B.T.Wakelam appeared in 1912, in a side which included Stoop, D.Lambert, Sibree, R.O.C. and H.G.Ward, and G.D.'Khaki' Roberts. Roberts, who had played for England in 1907 and 1908, later became an eminent barrister and KC.

The hazards of overseas matches were demonstrated in 1913. When the team ran out on the field at the Parc des Princes to play Stade Francais, they were greeted by admiring French girls throwing flowers. It would be by no means the last occasion when the Quins would be idolised to the point of embarrassment.

At the end of the 1913-14 season, when the Quins' last game at Twickenham had ended in a 38-4 victory over Bristol, few could have imagined that there would be no more Harlequin games for four years and that by the time they began again, many famous players would have been killed. We have mentioned Poulton-Palmer, but there were many more. Among them was A.F.Maynard, a burly second-row forward who had been capped three times in 1914. Maynard had scored an astonishing try when playing for Cambridge against Oxford (the match was then held at Queen's Club). Somebody had passed him the ball in midfield and, while looking anxiously from left to right for someone to pass to, he set off in the direction of the Oxford line. The thought that a lumbering forward could not go far on his own had occurred to several Oxford defenders, who therefore moved up to mark all those to whom it seemed he meant to pass. Wherever he looked, he could only see people in a worse position than himself, but as he went forward he was suddenly aware he was close to the Oxford line.

More surprised than anyone, he dived over and scored. Later he enlisted in the Royal Naval Division, survived the horrific beaches of Gallipoli in 1915, but was subsequently killed in France.

Lambert and 'Roc' Ward were also killed, and so too was Kenneth Powell an international hurdler. Kenneth Powell was also a Cambridge lawn tennis blue, of Wimbledon standard. Although a natural leader, Powell had joined the Honourable Artillery Company as a private in September 1914, because he wanted to get into action as soon as possible; he was killed a few months later.

On 27 September 1914, the club committee had a final meeting at which it was recorded that the balance sheet showed a profit of £276. A resolution was passed that this should be made up to £500 and the whole sum then be paid to the Prince of Wales' National Relief Fund. Subsequently, the Fund contributed to the building of the Star and Garter Home for disabled servicemen, which stands on Richmond Hill.

Although the war ended in November 1918, many of the surviving Harlequins were serving abroad and it was too late to arrange a programme of matches for the remainder of the 1918-19 season. However, it was decided that 1919-20 must show a return to pre-war standards. Fortunately those early investments had paid off and the Quins had a credit balance of £1,250. They also had the Twickenham agreement.

One of the club's pre-war members was H.B.T.Wakelam, mentioned earlier, who had joined the Quins in 1911. He had been up at Cambridge from 1911-14, but not won a blue. During the war he had served in various hazardous campaigns, including Gallipoli and France, been twice wounded, and mentioned in dispatches, and in 1918 he had been temporarily blinded by mustard gas. However, as soon as he was moderately fit he began playing again and in 1919 took on the post of club secretary, a position he held until 1923. Within that period he was also captain (1921-22). Wakelam, and others, realised that the top priority was recruiting promising players, and as a result R.Hamilton-Wickes, J.R.B.Worton, H.P.Marshall P.W.Adams and W.W.Wakefield came into the club.

At that time Wakefield was a young RAF officer, but his obvious talent for the game had caused him to be made both captain and honorary secretary of the RAF XV. Although only a junior officer, he had his own ideas on how Services rugger should be run, and believed that the only way to raise standards was to allow promising players to turn out for first-class club sides.

Inevitably, this policy provoked violent opposition from senior

A unique picture? Adrian Stoop on the field in 1912. Left to right: J.G.G.Birkett, H.J.Sibree, R.O.C.Ward, A.D.Stoop, an Oxford University player and G.R.Elmslie. Birkett played for England over twenty times, Sibree (scrum-half) three times. Elmslie was a three-quarter.

officers, who were short on experience and playing skills but long on opinion. *They* thought that RAF rugger players should take part in inter-unit and inter-service games only. The RAF was not alone in taking that view, which has persisted in all three Services over the years and still exists today. However, Wakefield, who had been reared in the north and educated in the spartan conditions of Sedbergh, was not prepared to sacrifice his principles and ideas to anyone. He therefore approached Lord Trenchard, then Chief of the Air Staff, and explained his view. Trenchard, no stranger to blinkered opposition in his own sphere, gave him full backing and as a result Wakefield produced an RAF XV which the following year won the Inter-Services Championship for the first time. Wakefield's membership of the Harlequins established a link with the RAF which has since brought the Harlequins many valuable recruits.

Wakelam, having helped to set the club on its feet again, was then dispatched by the Army to assist Maréchal Foch's special mission of transporting General Haller's Polish Army through Germany to Poland. After that, he resigned his Regular Commission, although maintaining his connection with the Army through a Territorial Commission in the Royal Engineers. In 1940 he was serving in the Middle East, although by that time he was forty-seven years old. He was subsequently invalided out, after being disabled, at the age of fifty-one. Long before World War Two he had become a household name from his radio broadcasts on rugger, soccer, cricket and lawn tennis. He gave the first running commentary ever broadcast in Britain, on the England v Wales match at Twickenham in 1927, and subsequently built up an audience of millions whom he treated as friends and equals. Similarly he was the 'voice' of all the Championship and Davis Cup lawn tennis matches from Wimbledon and Paris.

In 1938 he gave the first television commentary on a Test Match (England v Australia at Lord's). He was also a prolific author and the Rugby correspondent to the *Morning Post* (now merged with the *Daily Telegraph*). By his voice and his pen, Wakelam must have created more enthusiasm for Rugby Football (and other games) than anyone before or since. Among his better known book titles were *Twickenham Calling* and *And the Whistle's Gone*. He wrote an invaluable history of the Harlequins entitled *Harlequin Story*, which was published in 1954. Wakelam was undoubtedly a great Harlequin, who contributed enormously to the club. In spite of the effect of his wounds from World War One, he had continued playing as long as he could and captained an 'A' XV from 1924 to 1927.

But, in following individual careers, we have run ahead of our playing programme. The Quins' first game in 1919 was against Guy's Hospital. At that time, and for many years to come, Guy's was a leading first-class club, an achievement based on the fact that many talented South Africans used to go there for their medical studies. Part of the Guy's tactics was to give instructions in Afrikaans, on the basis that English rugger teams would be unlikely to understand it. The Harlequins solved the problem by playing a young South African who was serving in the Royal Artillery. He was said to be no great shakes as a player but was a first-class interpreter. The next match against Guy's ended in a narrow victory for the Harlequins. Since those days, the Quins have become used to contending with foreign languages on the field of play, not to mention all sorts of codes of numbers and passwords.

Two outstanding newcomers were now recruited by former players. One was V.G.Davies, a wing three-quarter who was known to G.V.Carey, and another was A.L.Gracie, a centre who was spotted by Maxwell-Dove when playing for his regiment in Germany. Gracie walked straight into the First XV and subsequently played thirteen times for Scotland. He was the first Quins' player to be the recipient of a very tempting offer from a Rugby League club which, needless to say, he declined. Gracie had the unusual distinction of being chaired off the field *by the Welsh* at Cardiff Arms Park, after he had scored a spectacular winning try against them in 1923. It says a lot for Gracie and even more for the sporting generosity of the Welsh.

This year saw a situation which must have been experienced by other clubs. Bristol thought the Quins were visiting them (and were right in thinking so), whilst the Quins thought the game was being staged at Twickenham. A hasty apologetic telegram cancelled the match and the Harlequins' fixture secretary resigned.

By 1920, the Quins were running three teams. In those days the 'A' teams were welcome visitors to schools and, as mentioned, were a useful channel for recruitment. This policy continued until the 1970s, when the Rugby Football Union issued an edict that men should not play against schoolboys. The loss of such traditional 'feeders' as Rugby, Eastbourne, Wellington, Marlborough, Tonbridge, Haileybury, Eton, Bedford, Radley, Felsted and Dulwich, to name but a few of the regular opponents of the schools 'A', has hit the Harlequins hard. However, like other clubs, the

Action from the 1920s. Note the scrum caps. Forwards who wanted to be noticed often wore white scrum caps!

Quins are now creating a new ladder to the top through colts and under-21 games. Of modern recruitment, more later.

The 1920-21 season was Wakefield's first year as captain of the club and it began with a 76-0 victory over Bedford. The Bedford club has suffered from some grievous defeats by the Harlequins, but always seems to rise from the ashes. However, the Quins had our own share of humiliation that year for an understrength First XV was beaten 36-0 by Guy's. The troubles were compounded by the fact that whilst the game was going on, someone was ransacking the Quins' dressing-rooms and removing all the loose cash. To add insult to injury, the thief walked off, quite literally, in the president's socks.

A rather more subtle performer, the author recalls, appeared before a game against Rosslyn Park (then at the Old Deer Park) in the Thirties. He carried a large tin box in which the Harlequins were invited to put their valuables 'for safe keeping'. Watches and wallets of various sizes then went into the receptacle which, it was assumed, would be put in a safe. After the game when enquiries were made for the man with the box, whom the Harlequins had imagined was a barman or groundsman, Rosslyn Park denied all knowledge of him. That must have been one of the soberest evenings a Harlequin team has ever spent.

The 1921-22 season saw the club in full swing again. Wakefield, who had been sent to Cambridge for two years by the RAF, captained the side. From time to time it included another Olympic hurdler, W.G.Tatham (who was also a talented musician). That season produced one of the most withering comments ever made about the club in a newspaper. The Quins visited Yorkshire for a weekend tour, playing Headingley on the Saturday and Otley on the Monday. Although both games ended in victory, the effects of Headingley's hospitality were still apparent on the Monday. A local scribe commented sourly on the Otley game: 'And now the Harlequins put on the decisive try, H.V.Brodie touching down after having broken all the written and most of the unwritten, laws of the game'.

In 1921 the Quins had a viscount (Encombe) making occasional appearances in the First XV. He was already an Oxford blue. He is said to have been the only viscount to have played first-class Rugby Football.

On 22 April 1922, a match entitled 'Harlequins Past v Harlequins Present' was played at Twickenham, the proceeds going to the King Edward VII Hospital Fund. Adrian Stoop captained the Past and had five other pre-war internationals to support him. They were his brother, F.M., and John Birkett, H.J.H.Sibree, G.D.Roberts, and A.H.McIlwaine.

In the 'Present' were Wakefield, A.L.Gracie, J.C.Gibbs, R.H.Hamilton-Wickes and V.G.Davies, of which all but Gibbs were already internationals and considerably shorter in the tooth than their opponents, a fact which brought them victory. As these words are being written, J.C.'Clifford' Gibbs is still Subscription treasurer of the club (at the age of 89).

On 9 February 1923, the club made history of a different sort by being the first full Rugby Football XV to fly to an overseas match. The destination was Cologne and the opponents were the British Army of the Rhine, who were defeated 45-3. The flight was memorable in more ways than one. Very few of the Harlequins had ever flown before when the two aircraft took off from Croydon, and by the time they had returned with the two pilots flying side by side and indulging in a few aerobatics, many more had decided never to do so again.

Consolidation

IN 1924, an American team played at Twickenham for the first time. It had arrived in Europe to represent America in the Olympic Games in Paris, where it won the tournament, although it must be said that neither England, Scotland, Wales nor Ireland were competing. When the Americans met the Harlequins, they were described by Wakelam as 'magnificent athletes and men of superb physique, and if the referee at times turned a blind eye to some of their obvious faults through ignorance, it was perhaps only his way of expressing his personal pleasure at their performance'. Be that as it may, the Harlequins defeated them 21-11.

Happily, the Quins had the great W.J.A.Davies playing for them in this match. Davies and his normal partner, C.A.Kershaw, are generally considered to have been one of the finest half-back combinations who have ever played for England. Both were in the Royal Navy and when not playing rugger together were as likely as not to be playing squash or some other game: hardly surprisingly they were said to read each other's thoughts.

Davies had won the first of his twenty-three caps in 1913, but was claimed for more important duties by the Navy for the next six years. When he turned out for the Harlequins he was in his last international season. Had his career not been interrupted by the war, his tally of caps could well have become an all-time record.

The Harlequins had now acquired a useful ground at Fairfax Road, Teddington. Although not perhaps as level as a perfectionist would have wished, it had the advantage that it was so well-drained it was playable under almost any weather conditions.

The 1924-25 season saw the arrival of the first All Blacks team since the war. They were a formidable proposition and included one of the 'all-time greats' in G.Nepia, the full-back. They came close to defeat when playing England at Twickenham, an occasion the club recalls with some pride as there were five Harlequins opposing the All Blacks on that day: W.W.Wakefield, H.J.Kittermaster, R.H.Hamilton-Wickes, V.G.Davies and J.C.Gibbs.

Clifford Gibbs had joined the Quins in September 1920, and

Harlequin FC 1923, the team that beat Bristol 16-10.

broken his left ankle in the very first trial game. When he had recovered a few months later, he wrote to the club and asked for a game as soon as there might be a vacancy. He was put in an 'A' XV, but, whilst in it, was selected to play for Kent at Blackheath. He scored five tries in that game and on the strength of it was chosen for the Harlequins' First XV against Richmond. He then played for the Firsts for ten more seasons. He would have liked to have retired earlier, but opposing clubs such as Bristol and Leicester asked if he could be included because his presence drew in the crowds and hence the gate money. He played alongside V.G. 'Bobby' Davies, mentioned above (who was killed by a bomb in World War Two), Philip Hodge, A.P.F.Chapman (the cricket captain of Kent and England), Harold Caccia (later Britain's

Harlequins v Cambridge University, 1923. Number four is Hamilton-Smythe, later to join the Quins. Note the tie holding up Cambridge shorts.

Ambassador in Washington), 'Bill' Gracie, and Douglas Bader. Caccia was a slender, red-headed Etonian of explosive temperament, and Douglas Bader the famous air ace of World War Two.

Bader was a highly-promising fly-half who later lost both his legs in a flying accident in 1931 but managed to get back into the RAF in 1939. Subsequently he shot down over twenty German aircraft and won the DSO twice and DFC twice. He was eventually shot down in France and, by a coincidence, it was J.C.Gibbs' squadron which dropped new artificial legs for him, after his originals had been damaged. Bader's determination to overcome the handicap of being legless later enabled him to become an excellent golfer and also to encourage many disabled people to become more mobile and achieve more than they had ever thought possible.

Clifford Gibbs recalls receiving so many passes out to the wing that on occasion they would beg the centres to run through themselves, while the wings got their breath back. When interviewed recently, Clifford Gibbs also recalled that Adrian Stoop ensured that the wing three-quarters had plenty of opportunity to run by getting the ball to them as quickly as possible. Stoop encouraged cross-kicks and short kicks ahead. Wakelam's comment on Gibbs was: 'Although light and rather fragile, he was one of the fastest ever of the Rugby world and, properly nursed and served, was capable of running around any defence.'

The fly-half of those days was H.J.Kittermaster. Like Gibbs, he was capped seven times for England. Kittermaster could take impossible passes, could kick, tackle and jink effectively, and was generally appreciated for the passes he gave, which pleased even Adrian Stoop. As mentioned, Adrian, although long past his peak, sometimes turned out for the Firsts in the Twenties. One of these occasions was a game against the London Welsh. The Harlequin scrum-half was John Worton, an Army player who eventually was capped twice for England. Before the game, Adrian Stoop took Worton on one side and gave him a series of code numbers designed to introduce unorthodox moves and baffle the Welsh. Worton, however, found this list of numbers more than he could manage, and on one occasion, when Stoop called out '432', he shook his head and called out, 'Sorry Adrian, number's engaged'.

In the Twenties the club had an embarrassingly large number of good players, making selection difficult. There were H.B.Style, a scrum half; I.J.Pitman (later MP for Bath), a forceful right wing who was capped in 1922; B.L.Jacot, an elegant dresser who was an almost unstoppable right wing (he was also a water-polo blue); and the two Price brothers, both Oxford blues and good all-rounders. Leo, who was capped four times for England at Rugby, was also a hockey blue and international, whilst his younger brother was captain of the Oxford cricket XI.

Howard Marshall, who would later become an even more famous radio commentator than Wakelam, also joined the club in the Twenties. Marshall's forte was describing cricket matches on the radio. When nothing was happening, as so often occurred, he would fill in the spare time with general observations. It was said that when Marshall was in front of the microphone he could make the listener see the grass growing. His soft, purring voice was ideal for his style. He was also an Oxford blue, who came near to getting an England cap. He played in the second row (lock) with R.R.Stokes, a Cambridge blue at both rugger and athletics and later an MP. Somewhat later, Marshall wrote an excellent book on Rugby Football in conjunction with W.W.Wakefield.

The pressure for First XV places in Twenties was of great benefit to the 'A's, who sometimes found themselves with an international

W.W.Wakefield wrestling for the ball against Old Millhillians in the 1928 Middlesex Sevens.

or two in their ranks. Players whose employment made it difficult for them to turn out regularly were often slotted into the 'A's, where they gave useful examples, and coaching, to the younger members. One such was W.F.R.Collis, a Cambridge blue who played seven times for Ireland but whose appearances for the Harlequins were restricted by his medical duties.

Another stalwart was G.W.'Bill' Haydon, a forceful wing who had been a member of the original British Expeditionary Force in 1914 and then twenty-five years later repeated the performance in 1939. He had been a lieutenant in the Middlesex Regiment in 1914, but by 1939 was a Lieutenant-Colonel commanding a battalion. He was killed in the Italian campaign.

In the *Daily Mail* for 4 February 1924, then a broadsheet newspaper the size of the present-day *Daily Telegraph,* there is an account of a Harlequin match against Northampton, which the Quins won 21-8. It is given as much space, on the same page, as the report of the Scotland-Wales match (which the former won 35-10).

Although J.C.Gibbs was playing for Kent v Somerset on that day and Gracie was not available either, the *Mail* reporter observed: 'The best that could be said of Northampton was that they put up a dogged fight. The Harlequin backs, with firm ground, dry ball, had every opportunity to enjoy themselves. The three-quarters gave a delightful exposition, straight running, cleverness, position kept, the ball passed and taken without slackening speed. And the "King and Lord of the line" was R.Hamilton-Wickes. As fine as his pace and sure handling was his judgement; as fine as his judgement was his tackling.'

In 1926 the first seven-a-side tournament was held at Twickenham. Happily, it was won by the Harlequins. Seven-a-side originated from the Scottish Border clubs (Melrose has the honour of having invented them) where local conditions made it difficult at times to raise a full XV. The competition was brought to London by a Scottish referee, J.C.Russell-Cargill, who was a doctor at Middlesex Hospital. The proceeds go to Middlesex Charities.

The Harlequin VII was: J.C.Gibbs, R.Hamilton-Wickes, V.G.Davies, J.R.B.Worton, W.W.Wakefield, W.F.Browne, and J.S.Chick, all but Chick being internationals. The Final, against St Mary's Hospital, was won by 25-3. It was said, 'All you had to do was to give the ball to Gibbs and lie down while he scored'. The Middlesex Sevens have, of course, been won by the Harlequins many times since and, at the time of writing, the trophy is still in the club's possession, having been won for a record number of consecutive times. The event now attracts nearly as many people as international matches.

The Quins proceeded to win the Sevens again the following year, this time defeating Blackheath 28-6 in the Final, and then for the next two years also. In those days a try counted for three points and a conversion added another two. Penalty goals were

The 1926 Maoris demonstrating their 'haka' at Twickenham prior to being defeated 11-5 by the Quins.

worth three points and a dropped goal counted for four. There was much agonising when a team which had scored a try was beaten by a dropped goal in the last minute, after they had hung on to what they had thought was a winning lead for most of the game.

The Maoris had also appeared in 1926, complete with their preliminary 'Haka' which is now demonstrated by all New Zealand teams. The Maoris were primarily on a tour of France, where they played most of their matches. However, the Quins beat them 11-6 in a hard fought game at Twickenham.

Various unusual characters appeared in a Harlequin jersey in the Twenties. One was a Japanese prince, who was visiting Britain to learn about English games. He played at centre three-quarter in the schools 'A', as he was rather light, and had in his first game the misfortune to suffer from a dressing-room thief. The other Harlequins lost little of value, but the Japanese was carrying a substantial sum of money and a gold watch. He had to be reassured that the theft was not a normal feature of English Rugby Football.

Action from the 1926 game against the Maoris.

Another unusual member was S.J.Rossdale. Rossdale, who came to the Harlequins via Clifton and Trinity Hall, Cambridge, was not a particularly skilful player and therefore languished long in the 'A's. He was, however, immensely strong, so much so that when he once encountered that formidable international forward A.F.Blakiston, he threw his opponent right over his head. Rossdale was one of those people, usually taken for granted, who spared no efforts in administration and other behind-the-scenes chores.

The closing years of the decade saw the Harlequins including a French international fly-half named André Verger. He was one

J.C.Gibbs tackling a United Services player.

Quins defeating the London Scottish at Twickenham in the 1920s. Shorts scarcely deserved their name in that era.

of many French guests whom the Quins have been pleased to welcome to the club.

H.C.G.Laird also made his debut, and won the first of his ten international caps, against Wales, in 1927. Colin Laird had the unusual ability of being able to kick equally, and exceptionally, well, with either foot, although he favoured the left.

J.C.Hubbard (eighty-nine years old at the time of writing) had come to the Harlequins from Tonbridge in 1925. He had originally planned to join Blackheath, which his father had played for (as well as for England in the 1890s), but been told he was not really good enough to get into any of their 'A' teams. Disappointed, he turned to Adrian Stoop to ask if he would have more luck with the Harlequins. Adrian took note and, as a result, Jack Hubbard became the Quins' rock-solid full-back and was capped for England in 1930. On wet days he used to wear mittens. Surprisingly, mittens seem to have disappeared from sight these days, although the cold wet days which justified them are still with us.

Among those winning caps in the Twenties were J.W.R.Swayne (England), one of three brothers who came from Bromsgrove in Worcestershire; J.S.Synge, a Cambridge blue who appeared for Ireland; and J.S.R.Reeve. Reeve, who had learnt the game at Rugby, went on to Cambridge but never won a blue: however, he played eight times for England, the first time when he was still at Cambridge. He was a tall, long-striding, wing whose style baffled friend and foe alike, for he appeared to leave both behind as he made his determined way to the line. He did exactly this against Wales in 1930, going through the whole Welsh side. A barrister, he was also a good hurdler and cricketer.

The Twenties had been a remarkable decade. With the arrival of Wakefield, the pre-war reputation of the Harlequin club was rebuilt and, with Adrian Stoop to keep a paternal eye on matters, the Harlequin style of play was preserved and improved.

The Thirties

ALTHOUGH the Harlequin club maintained a satisfactory playing record in the Thirties, the same cannot be said for its financial position. Reserves took a steep dive in 1931, the first year of the world slump which had followed the American stock market crash of 1929. Overall the club lost £1,600, which in today's currency values would be a substantial sum. A timely legacy from a former Harlequin captain (1892-93). A.B.Cipriani, gave the Harlequins £600, which included a Teddington £100 debenture.

In 1930, J.C.Hubbard was playing full-back for England, and P.W.P.Brook, a Cambridge blue, obtained the first of his three caps, of which the last came in 1936. Peter Brook was a large, genial, wing forward who took Holy Orders and was the chaplain of Clifton College for many years. He recalled that in one of his early games he was suddenly punched, for no reason, by Ken Chapman. Turning indignantly, he said: "What on earth was that for?" Imperturbably, Chapman replied: "Because it will make you sulk and you always play better when you are sulking."

Peter Brook taught many promising rugger players at Clifton, among them R.A.M.Whyte, D.G.Perry and the Forbes brothers. J.E.Hutton was capped for Scotland (and played against some of his Harlequin comrades in 1930). He was capped again, against France the following year.

In 1931, the Harlequins gained three more international recognitions. One was for their dimunitive scrum-half, G.J.'Tinny' Dean. Like Reeve, he had failed to get a blue at Cambridge but had a thriving career with the Harlequins and the Army. He was in the Royal Tank Regiment and this was thought by many to be entirely appropriate, for he seemed to be almost as indestructible as an ironclad. Dennis Swayne, an Oxford blue and a doctor, was not available to the club as often as he would have wished, but was a man whose contribution to the social side of the club was valued almost as much as his playing performances.

P.E.Dunkley (no relation to F.P., who came later) was a hefty wing-forward who eventually won six caps. 'Pop' Dunkley also

England scrum-half J.B.Worton (Harlequins) passing in a game against Richmond in 1932.

played for Warwickshire in a successful team in which he was sometimes the only member who did not come from the Coventry club. He was a bank manager. Somewhat unusually for a rugger player he was a teetotaller. He was also deeply religious and a keen supporter of Toc H, the organisation for social and religious welfare which had been founded by the Revd Tubby Clayton, during the middle of World War One. Above the doorway of the premises in Poperinghe were the words 'Abandon rank all ye who enter here'. Over 20,000 soldiers used it as a refuge and temporary relief from the horrors of the trenches a few miles away near Ypres. Adrian Stoop was a friend of Tubby Clayton.

R. 'Reg' Bolton was another storming wing-forward; he played for England on and off for five years. He had begun his rugger career at Queen Elizabeth's Grammar School, Wakefield, at the age of seven, and played three times a week until he left at the age of eighteen. By that time, he had also joined Wakefield RFC and played for Yorkshire. Whilst a medical student, he played for his hospital in London but went back to Yorkshire to play for

63

C.Thompson tackling E.J.Unwin (Army) in 1933 (see page 66).

the county. He was picked for England in 1933. 'This was the disastrous match against Wales when they won at Twickenham for the first time,' he recalls. Although Bolton was picked as a wing-forward, he was taken out of the scrum and put on the wing when one of the English three-quarters (R.A.Gerrard) was injured. There were, of course, no replacements allowed in those days, so England played most of this match one short. Bolton apparently played quite well as a substitute wing three-quarter but was dropped for the next game. R.F.Oakes, the Yorkshire secretary, told him that now he was in London he should join the Harlequins and try to get back into the England side.

'I didn't know anything about the Quins,' said Bolton, 'apart from their reputation as a top élitist club, full of Oxford and Cambridge blues. I was somewhat worried about my reception but I found this was groundless and was received with open arms by a good backbone of North Country and Midlands. To name a few, the Chapman brothers, Joe Mycock, Fred and Philip Dunkley, Brian Gray, Noel McGrath, Norman Steel, all country bumpkins. I spent very happy years there till the war. In my playing days all First XV games were at Twickenham and so we never had any contact, social or otherwise, with the 'A' team at Teddington, who seemed miles away and we hadn't even got motor-cars. The disadvantage was that I never met the bulk of the players as the Quins didn't have any routine evening training. I am told that from this aspect the Stoop Ground is a great improvement. Were the Quins fit? I think so. We usually did our own training and ran round Regent's Park every morning at 7am.

'We were all very poor but enjoyed every minute. There seems too much money about now but I won't go into that. I was, and am, an amateur.'

During World War Two, Bolton was blown up by a German bomb in Naples harbour but subsequently returned to take part in the social activities of the Quins. He was in excellent form at the unveiling of the Chapman portrait at the Stoop on 23 February 1991.

The Prescott family came on to the Harlequin scene in the Thirties. They were the sons of Ernest Prescott, a leading figure in Rugby Union administration; he had married the sister of the redoubtable C.E.L.'Curly' Hammond (see above) in the early years of the century. R.E.'Robin' was an Oxford blue who graduated into an England front-row forward. Like many another player he had his playing career cut short by World War Two but by the time it broke out he had already won six caps. Robin was a lawyer who eventually became secretary of the Rugby Union, but also found time to do an enormous amount of administrative work for the club. He exuded an air of quiet geniality, except when he was playing in the front row, of course. His brother, A.E.C. 'Tony', likewise an Oxford blue, did yeoman service for the club, although he never quite rose to the playing heights of his brother.

The Thirties saw various interesting players floating in and out of the club. One of these was F.L. Hovde, an American wing three-quarter who, in the days when wing three-quarters used to throw in from touch, had a novel (to us) style. Instead of bowling the ball over his head, or lobbing it underhand, as was the prevalent English custom, he launched it, American fashion, like a spinning torpedo. Many players tried to copy his style, with considerably less success.

The Harlequin back-row in the Thirties was frequently Reg Bolton, Peter Brook and Edward 'Ham' Hamilton-Hill. Ham, who was in the Royal Navy, was capped three times. This combination of three internationals was a fearful sight to the opposing halves and three-quarters, as in those days, as previously mentioned, the activities of marauding breakaway forwards were much less restrained by referees. Periodically there were shouts from the stands that the wing-forward should do more shoving in the scrums, but these pleas were invariably ignored as were also complaints in letters to the *Times* and *Daily Telegraph* that wing-forwards were destroying constructive three-quarter play. Many back-row forwards would begin to break as soon as the ball was put in the scrum. The Rugby Union, in one of its periodic wrestling matches with the laws, produced the astonishing rule that the back row forwards of the side which had won the ball should not break until the ball was out of the scrum, thus completely failing to check the real villains, the wing-forwards on the other side.

Other notable forwards in the Thirties included Chris Thompson, who had an England trial before going out to join the Malayan Civil Service. When Japan invaded Malaya, Thompson, who had enlisted in the Federation Volunteer Force, was taken prisoner and eventually died of malnutrition on the infamous Burma-Siam railway. J.H. Steeds, a front-row forward who had won a blue at Cambridge, also joined the Harlequins in the Thirties. During World War Two, when he was a doctor in the Navy, he broke his jaw in one accident and his neck in another, but recovered to achieve the remarkable feat of being capped for England five times as a hooker; there cannot be many players who have won

S.A.Block, seen here playing against the Army in 1933, gained Cambridge cricket and hockey blues, but not rugger.

international caps in the front row after having previously broken their necks.

There was an abundance of strong-running backs at this point, a fact of considerable value in the Quins' seven-a-side game. Among these were A.G.'Geoff' Butler, who was capped twice for England in 1937; G.E.C.Hudson, a centre who often caught the eye but never capped; and J.D.Ronald. Ronald was an enterprising full-back who was later killed while serving in the RAF. There were

R.E.Prescott (10) stopping a Bath player in 1933. Quins won 19-9.

two promising three-quarters in the brothers Chapman. Rather surprisingly they were the sons of Herbert Chapman, a famous and successful manager of the Arsenal Association Football Club. However, both his sons had been at school at St Peter's, York (which had Guy Fawkes as one of its earlier pupils) and had played Rugby Football (and many other games) successfully there.

J.B.D. (Bruce) seemed likely to go further but had to give up the game through injury. K.H. 'Ken' was a good all-rounder and useful cricketer but spent most of his early days in the 'A's. Eventually, increasing size and weight made him decide to become a forward and in that position he became part of a very solid First XV engine-room. Not least of his assets was the ability to place-kick with great length and accuracy. As a forward he captained the club in 1936, 1937, 1938 and 1945. Subsequently he became president. Ken, who was a solicitor by profession, had an imperturbable, genial, personality. Few people have worked more assiduously for the Harlequin club. He had begun his career as an administrator as team secretary for the 'A's in 1932; after the war, in 1945, he was unsparing in his efforts to put the club on its feet again.

S.A.Block, a Cambridge cricket and hockey, though not rugger, blue, was often the Quins' full-back in the Thirties; J.R.Rawlence, a Cambridge blue in 1936 and 1937, also played for the club. Rawlence achieved a form of fame in the 1936 University match when he was going hard for the Oxford line and was apparently certain to score. However, Oxford had Prince Alex Obolensky playing for them on the opposite wing that day and 'Oboe', who could run as fast in rugger boots as he could on the running track, came across at tremendous speed and intercepted Rawlence with a devastating tackle.

Possibly because of the Adrian Stoop tradition, the Harlequins have never suffered a dearth of stand-off halves. In the late Thirties, the club could call on Ian Watts, who had won a blue at Oxford, T.G.K.Bishop, and W.S.Kemble. Tom Bishop joined the Lancashire Fusiliers in World War Two, won a Military Cross, and was shot through the femoral artery in Italy. Normally a wound in the femoral artery gives a man under two minutes to live, but those who knew Tom Bishop were not surprised to hear that, miraculously, he had survived, although he never played rugger again.

Although generally considered one of the most maverick characters ever to play for the club, the centre of almost every escapade before or after the war, Bishop had another side to his character. He was extremely musical, a superb piano player and also a highly-knowledgeable countryman, an expert on trees, plants, birds, soils etc and was very good with animals. Children regarded him as an inexhaustible source of entertainment, information and wise counsel.

Sam Kemble had come to the Harlequins via Moseley and Cambridge, and had been given an England trial. He took Holy Orders and became a prison chaplain. It was said that it must have been bad enough to be in prison, without having Kemble to stir you up; undoubtedly he was a very conscientious parson when it came to saving souls.

T.H.Tilling was another regular three-quarter in this era. He came via Tonbridge (which has contributed many players to the club, notably David Marques, Jack Hubbard, Derek Whiting among others) and was a barrister. However, Humphrey Tilling was also a gifted amateur actor who was a driving force in 'The Old Stagers', a distinguished dramatic society which dated from 1842. He acted, managed, wrote scripts and directed. There was nothing 'amateur' about the performances. He also played cricket for Surrey Second XI and, later, his magnificent voice gave him the role of narrator for the annual Festival of Remembrance at the Albert Hall.

Their close liaison with Oxford and Cambridge served the Harlequins in good stead. Undergraduates who had won blues regarded playing for the Quins as a possible step to an international cap; those who had not so far achieved blues regarded playing for the Harlequins as a helpful step towards getting one. In the early Thirties, the Quins had two very useful hookers from Oxford, L.R.H.Leach and J.Hudson. Neither looked remotely likely to get a blue because E.S.Nicholson, an England international, was firmly established in that position in the Oxford pack. The club took a benign view of the University members, who appreciated being paid their railway fares plus 2s 6d for lunch, whether they were playing for the First, the First 'A', or any other team the Quins happened to be running at the time.

In the Thirties, the postal services were considerably quicker and more reliable than they are today. Team secretaries could post a double (reply-paid) postcard on Sundays and the recipient would see: 'You have been selected to play against . . .' and directions for travelling. The player would then tear off the other half, sign it saying 'Yes' or 'No', and post it back. Sometimes there would be so many refusals, because of injury or otherwise, that a fresh flight of cards might need to be sent in midweek.

Rugby Football in London in the Thirties became very inbred. Harlequins, Blackheath and Richmond were happy to play each other home and away and the same applied to the Quins' fixtures with Oxford and Cambridge. London Scottish were regarded as suitable opponents, but London Welsh and London Irish were felt to be less strong. That situation changed later.

The Quins played Rosslyn Park, but the Park was not regarded as very firmly situated in the upper ranks. There were also games against Guy's Hospital, Old Merchant Taylor's and Aldershot Services, all of whom have long disappeared from the Harlequin's First XV fixture list. United Services, Portsmouth, were a regular fixture, as were Cardiff, Newport and Swansea. From the Midlands, the Quins played Northampton and Leicester, but not Coventry, formidable though that club was with its seven internationals.

In the Thirties, although the idea of a league, or even a knock-out cup, would have been regarded with shocked horror, an unofficial ranking list certainly operated. The word 'élitism' had not gained its current popularity but it was a governing factor. In contrast, the arrival of the cup and the league, although creating a formal order of strength, has widened the fixture list considerably. Like other clubs, who have been knocked out of the cup, the Quins have often had to scratch around to find a fixture. In the 1980s,

Harlequins beat London Welsh 10-3 in the Final of the Middlesex Sevens in 1935. Standing (left to right): G.E.C.Hudson, E.Hamilton-Hill, P.E.Dunkley, P.W.P.Brook, A.G.Butler. On ground: G.J.Dean, J.R.Cole.

one of these was Nuneaton, who had been in existence for over a hundred years, were a first-class club, but had never played against the Harlequins. Unfortunately for them, on the day the Quins met them for the first time, the Harlequins had two star All Blacks as guests playing for them; even then, the Quins managed to beat them only by a few points.

An advantage of cup and league matches has been the appearance fo fresh faces at Twickenham and the Stoop, which provides extra interest for spectators, and also makes the Harlequins aware of the background of some of their recruits. In pre-cup and league days, if a player joined the Harlequins from a club the Quins had never played, he was unlikely, unless lucky, to get a trial in the First XV. It is, of course, a fact that the Harlequins only accept playing members who are considered to be of potential First XV standard. This has always been their principle and for this reason the Quins have never run more than a few teams, usually a First, a Second (Wanderers), and not more than two 'A's. (These have

K.H.Chapman, captain of the club in 1938. He was a son of Herbert Chapman, the great Arsenal soccer manager.

Adrian Stoop in 1936, chatting to Engineer Commander S.F.Cooper (secretary of the Rugby Union).

now been joined by the highly successful under-21 (Jaguars) and the Colts, both grooming players for the senior teams.)

With this policy operating, many of the Wanderers, Jaguars and 'A' team players have played regularly in County sides and on occasion a player from the Wanderers (or First 'A') has won an international cap. Today, when players are watched in training, and captains are more concerned with identifying and advancing talented players than in keeping the same team together, the Quins are unlikely to repeat the mistakes of the past.

We mentioned that from time to time the Harlequins have had fixtures with Germany. According to Wakelam, the Quins also had a German member in the Thirties. His account of this follows:

'In 1935, a German, one Fritz Gruenebaum, was elected to the club. He was over here as a student and was a most amusing and entertaining companion, his repertoire of the traditional drinking songs of his country and his melodious tenor voice enlivening many a train journey or party. Though not of First XV calibre, he was soon well known in the club and often one wondered vaguely what had happened to him after September 1939.

'We were then represented at centre three-quarter by K.S. (Ken) Robinson. A Territorial Army subaltern when the war broke out, Ken went over to France for the D-Day landings (1944), commanding a light ack-ack battery of Bofors guns, being with the spearhead of the advance right across, and reaching Kiel as the German surrender came. He was then ordered to take charge of the many thousands of German prisoners who were pouring back from the Russian front, and one very considerable party of these men seemed somewhat difficult and obstreperous. At the request of his sergeant-major, Ken went across to see what he could do, to be faced by a smartly turned-out German staff major who, having saluted punctiliously, suddenly said in English: "Aren't you Ken Robinson, the Harlequin centre?" It was, of course, Fritz, and after that there was no more trouble.' Gruenebaum is alive, lives in the USA, and is still a member.

Among the influx of Oxford players were H.D.Freakes, R.M.Marshall and M.M.Walford. Freakes was a South African who qualified in his three years at Oxford, where he won three blues. Originally a full-back, he was brought into the Oxford three-quarter line to 'neutralise' the brilliant Cambridge attacking centres in 1937. His companion in that marathon of tackling was

Opposite: Harlequins v Rosslyn Park in 1939.
Prince Obolensky hands-off a Harlequin who
has misjudged his tackle. He was not the only
one to misjudge Obolensky's speed.

September 1939 and an early wartime match. The Harlequin making the tackle is J.Bush.

M.M.Walford, and those who watched it said they had never seen tackling with such deadly accuracy ever before. Freakes played three times for England and was, alas, killed in the war. Walford was never capped, although he too played for Oxford for three years. Walford had arrived at Oxford from Rugby, having played for the school 112 times at various games, and proceeded to distinguish himself at Oxford by winning blues for hockey and cricket as well as rugger. Later he became a housemaster at Sherborne.

Marshall won three England caps, but, had he survived the war, in which he served in the Royal Navy, he would undoubtedly have won many more, for he was one of the best forwards ever to wear a Harlequin jersey. Three other internationals of those days were B.E.Nicholson, M.J.Daley, and F.J.V.Ford, the first playing for England twice, Daly appearing for Ireland once and Ford for Wales once.

World War Two, as we have seen, took a heavy toll of Rugby footballers who, perhaps inevitably, were in the front of much of the action. In connection with a war which caused so many deaths and so much misery and desolation world-wide, it may seem a trivial point to mention the effect it had on the playing careers of Rugby footballers; nevertheless it should not pass unrecorded that promising players who were reaching their peak in 1939 were then ruled out of top-level Rugby Football for the next six years. There were, of course, inter-unit matches and one or two representative matches, but no one in his right mind took the idea of wartime 'blues' or wartime 'internationals' seriously: they were tokens, no more, no less. The hard facts were that a player in his early twenties at the start of the war would be long past his potential peak by the end of it, even if he was not affected by wounds or other afflictions. Even so, quite a few players managed to make some sort of comeback.

From those who were still in England in early 1944, the Quins managed to raise an all-Harlequins team in April of that year. It included one or two 'veterans', such as J.D.Ronald, M.M.Walford, and some youngsters who were going to give the Harlequins valuable service in the future. Among these last were P.R.H.Hastings, F.P.Dunkley, B.H.Bowring, J.R.C.Matthews and D.K.Brooks. Both Johnny Matthews, at that time a surgeon-lieutenant in the Royal Navy, and David Brooks, a Fleet Air Arm pilot, would later captain the club. The Rosslyn Park team was also, unknowingly, supplying the Harlequins with future members, for it included H.G.Thomas, H.de Lacey, D.B.Vaughan, B.H.McGuirk, and C.D.McIver.

Apart from this game, the Quins played a few others in partnership with Rosslyn Park but no records of the matches, or opponents, seem to have survived.

Rebuilding

SOMEWHAT optimistically, the club held a meeting on 25 July 1945 at St Stephen's Tavern, Westminster Bridge, and made arrangements for the coming season. The war in Europe was, of course, over, having finished on 7 May, but it seemed to have escaped attention that the conflict in the Far East was continuing and, with five million fanatical Japanese soldiers still under arms, the final stages looked like being bloody and protracted. In the event, Japan capitulated after receiving two atomic bombs, and the Far Eastern war ended on 15 August 1945.

Even then, many Harlequins were still engaged in duties overseas and would continue to be so, as long as they were required, on garrison tasks in Germany, Italy, Austria and many other countries. Nevertheless, it was a good idea to make a start. Remarkably, three members of the committee which had met and restarted the club after World War One were also present on this occasion. They were H.B.T.Wakelam, E.M.C.Clarke and H.E.Ward, the long-serving treasurer.

Adrian Stoop, who combined the offices of president and secretary, was chairman. Ken Chapman was elected captain again and also took on the duties of secretary of the First XV which, of course, meant arranging fixtures. Harold Clarke was elected captain of the 'A' which, initially, was the only other team the Quins ran. Arranging fixtures was likely to be a problem for the other clubs, which were also starting up again, and were also having problems. Richmond and Blackheath were running a combined team at that time. Not surprisingly, it was called Richmond-Blackheath. A number of junior clubs, stiffened by neighbouring services personnel, were quite strong at that time: Twickenham was one of them. D.B.Willis took on the responsibility for nursemaiding the 'A's. Derek was a front-row forward who had played for the First XV in the Thirties and continued to give loyal service to the club for many years to come.

Among 'those present' were Colin Laird, Norman Steel, Peter Adams and Richard Hamilton-Wickes.

Financially the Quins were in a sound position, with assets worth

Harlequins' First XV in 1945, the first season after World War Two. Back row (left to right): Vaughan, Brooks, Horner, Hudson, Weighill, Lemon, Cooke. Middle row: Barton, De Lacey, Chapman, Adrian Stoop, Dunkley, Birkett. Front row: Bulmer, Steele-Bodger, Butler.

£5,000. They had the lease on Twickenham and plenty of space at Teddington. As they were demobilised, many former players made contact with the club. There was J.D.(John) Miller, who had spent the war with the Fleet Air Arm, E.K.Scott, B.D.Napper A.G.Butler, S.G.Fowler, D.Bulmer and S.H.Dowse. Basil Napper had arrived from Marlborough with a great reputation in the mid Thirties, but did not achieve a regular place in the First XV until 1945. He captained the team, as a full-back, in 1946.

Geoff Butler had joined the club in 1932 as a schoolboy from Henley. He was a wing three-quarter with an electrifying burst of speed, which is hardly surprising in view of the fact that he became an international sprinter and also won the Southern Counties 'double' in the 100 and 220 yards. In 1963 he was president of the Rugby Football Union and in that capacity raised an all-international team to play the Harlequins on 7 September 1963.

Being president of the RFU must have seemed an unlikely prospect for Geoff Butler when he played for the First XV on 14

February 1934. The opponents on that day were Eastbourne (the town, not the college), the referee was G.V.Carey and the Quins' team included such stalwarts as Robin Prescott, Dennis Swayne, Bruce Chapman and another flying wing called H.L.V.Faviell. Even so, the Quins appear to have had to fight strenuously to defeat opponents who nowadays have slipped down to being a fixture for the First 'A' team.

Butler still has the fixture card for his first season with the club, which was 1932-33. One of the vice-presidents was the Bishop of Labuan (Borneo). One feels he cannot have attended many matches. P.E.Dunkley was captain of the Firsts in that year and Ken Chapman, H.J.Gould, and C.R.Hinds Howell captained the 'A's. In that season the First XV played certain other teams which have now dropped a few stages in the Quins' fixture list, or have even been lost altogether. They included Sandhurst (though not Woolwich), O.M.T.s, St Bartholomew's Hospital, Guy's Hospital and the Old Millhillians.

Today the idea of an Old Boys' team being able to take on the Harlequins' First XV may seem inconceivable, but the best of the Old Boys' sides were a formidable proposition, often possessing one or two internationals. In the early Thirties, the Old Millhillians had a pair of international half-backs, W.S.Sobey and R.S.Spong, who could be guaranteed to set any match alight. In the Fifties, the Quins acquired an excellent scrum-half from the Old Millhillians, J.E.Williams, who won eight international caps.

The 1933 'A' XV fixture list is illuminating. It included a large number of schools: Haileybury, Radley, Wellington, Tonbridge, Rugby, Marlborough, Felsted, St Edward's, Canford, Brighton, Oratory and Eastbourne, but also a large number of Army teams: the Guards Depot, Duke of Wellington's, Welsh Guards, Scots Guards, Welch Regiment and the RASC. Most of the Army teams were brawny rather than skilful and, although they could usually push the Harlequin forwards off the ball in the set scrum, they were no match for the Quins' fleet-footed three-quarters.

Having served his apprenticeship in the 'A's, Butler became a regular in the First XV and was capped for England in 1937. He linked up again with the club in 1945 and was soon racing down the wing again, and continued to do so for several years.

Jay Gould was another long-serving loyal member of the club. As mentioned above, he had captained one of the 'A's in the early Thirties, and was in and out of the First XV. Eventually he became secretary to the club and discharged his duties in that onerous post with commendable zeal and efficiency. Jay was also a talented

Harlequins in 1946. Basil Napper is the captain.

impromptu actor who took a leading part in Harlequin 'theatricals'.

Ian Watts, the Oxford fly-half, also came back to the Quins. They also had Maurice Daly, an Irish international, who could play anywhere behind the scrum but flourished on the wing, and H.de Lacey, who would play for Ireland in 1948. At full-back they had the versatile J.M.H.Roberts, who was a Welsh Guardsman, and Welsh trial cap.

In 1946, Ken Chapman relieved Adrian Stoop of the duties of being secretary, which, as Adrian had held the post for forty years, seemed about due. Nevertheless, Adrian continued as the Harlequins' president and advisor.

By 1946 the Quins were already stocking up with internationals. One of them was M.R.Steele-Bodger, who subsequently became president of the RFU. 'Micky' Steele-Bodger was a wing-forward, who made up in speed and mobility what he lacked in size. He was eventually capped nine times for England. He had arrived in the club via Cambridge University and Moseley.

B.H.Travers, an Australian, arrived after winning two blues at Oxford, and went on to win six English caps, one of them against

The Quins' First XV, 1947-8: Back row (left to right) Referee (partly hidden), Butler, Pigot, Stileman, Hudson, Grimsdell, Roberts, Weston, Horner, Devine. Middle row: Plumtree, Dunkley, Matthews, Adrian Stoop, Daly, Brooks (who is the 1991 president). On ground: Bellamy, De Lacey.

his native Australia. 'Jika' Travers had a reputation for having built up his strength by eating several scrum-halves for breakfast.

Chris Horner remembers his first encounter with Jika Travers when the Quins were playing Oxford University at Twickenham on 16 February 1946. 'I was jumping for the ball in the line-out. Up to now this had been working well but each time I was being barged off the ball. Being quite a novice with the Quins, I had a word with the man of experience, our captain, then Chapman, who told me to go to the back of the line-out while he dealt with this chap. At the next line-out there was a scuffle and a body on the ground. Good old Ken, I thought, that's fixed the so and so, but to my horror the body on the ground was Ken with a nasty split lip and a black eye. Getting up, he mumbled, "OK Chris, that's fixed it, you can take over again".'

Subsequently, Chris (C.M.Horner) often found himself playing alongside Travers in the Harlequin pack. Among Horner's souvenirs of his playing days is the programme for the game against

Bristol on 5 November 1949. Before the match the two captains placed a wreath on the war memorial plaque at the entrance to the Bristol ground. A trumpeter then sounded the *Last Post* and *Reveille*. The plaque was in memory of the Rugby players of Bristol who had given their lives in the two wars.

In the programme was a tribute to the Quins, which, coming from our great rivals and friends, merits printing here:

> *It is fitting that the Harlequins should visit us on Armistice Day, for those of us who knew Rugby before 1914 will recall the great Harlequin XV of those days. To watch them was a delight, to play against them was a revelation. The experience was a wholesome discipline, for lessons so painfully learnt were not easily forgotten. Nowadays many a club calling itself first-class has but one player of real international calibre. The Harlequins of those days had fifteen such players, directed by Adrian Stoop. May we see some Rugby of real Harlequin quality this afternoon.*

In another Bristol programme appeared the words:

> *The Harlequins play the game as it should be played. They have no liking for crafty evasions of the laws or matching their wits against those of the referee. They realise, as do all good rugger men, that the Laws of Rugby do not legislate for the cheat and it is easily possible to beat the law. When the Harlequins see the ball they pick it up and run with it and are loath to kick it. May they continue for many years to visit us.*

Thank you Bristol, for these kind words. We have the same respect and admiration for you.

The year 1950 saw the debut of R.M.Bartlett, whose immense contribution to the club, both on and off the field, would last many years. Ricky, a fly-half who had learnt the game at Stowe, was a quiet, unobtrusive person. He first played for the Harlequins when still at school, from which he went on to Cambridge, and won a blue in 1951. By the end of the decade he would have seven England caps. One of his specialities was the quick kick ahead and to the wing. When J.R.C.Young, an Oxford blue and international sprinter was playing, either for the Harlequins or England (for which he won eight caps) Ricky's perfectly positioned kicks meant an almost certain score. Ricky, who died at a tragically early age, never spared himself. The author recalls seeing him touch-judging at the Stoop on a bitterly cold day and then coming in immediately after the game to begin serving in the bar, although literally blue with cold. He had no sense of self-importance and would turn out in all sorts of games, preferably charitable ones for good causes. Truly, a great Harlequin.

But in looking at Ricky Bartlett's career we have bypassed a number of other players who made a substantial contribution to the re-establishment of the club in the post-war era. Some of them spanned World War Two. Maurice Daly was a case in point. Although at his best on the wing, Daly was a very useful stand-off half where he was often partnered by H.de Lacy, an Irish international. Daly recalled playing in a game at Leicester, where he encountered a referee of the dour, no-nonsense, variety. On one of the drop-outs, Daly decided to kick diagonally away from the forwards and thus catch the opposite side at a disadvantage. To his astonishment, he heard a piercing blast on the whistle as the referee bore down on him. 'Take that properly,' said the referee, who was apparently unaccustomed to the subtleties of the game. 'We don't want any of your West End tricks here.'

We hope that referee lived to see some of the brilliant deceptive ploys of Leicester fly-halves of the last few decades who revelled in the unorthodox.

The late Forties' sides included Ken Chapman, who although getting a bit long in the tooth was still a powerful factor in the engine room and a prodigious long-distance kicker. A.A.(Alan) Grimsdell appeared and would be joined later by his brother W.R.'Billy'. N.A. (Norman) Steel often appeared at scrum-half and for a time the Quins also had the services of J.A.Davies, a Welsh wartime international who varied between fly-half and centre three-quarter. The left wing position was usually taken by D.M.(David) Stileman, an Army player. David's family have been among the club's most supportive members.

Since the days of Wakefield, the Quins have always had close links with the RAF. Air Commodore R.G.H.Weighill appeared in 1946 and went on to win several England caps; later he was secretary of the RFU. Roy Austen-Smith later became an Air Marshal and K.B.B. (Sir Kenneth) Cross an Air Chief Marshal. P.B.Lucas, the distinguished golfer, was also a member. Also from the RAF were R.J.H.Uprichard, who went on to win two Irish caps in 1950, E.L.Horsfall, who was capped against Wales in 1949, and Wing-Commander John Seldon, another long-standing member who is now a vice-president. Alan Grimsdell was a pilot, all 6ft 5in of him, which can't have left much room for anyone else in his aircraft.

R.T.'Reggie' Kindred was particularly unfortunate, for he was shot down over Brest and lost a leg. However, he has never allowed this disablement to interfere in the slightest degree with the invaluable work he has done for the club, as chairman and in many other capacities.

In an earlier generation the Quins had Air Commodore J.S.Chick, MC, AFC. An excellent wing-forward, he had an English trial but just missed being capped. He was an outstanding pilot, won the MC in 1918, and later commanded the high-speed flight in the Schneider Trophy races.

G.E. (Gerry) Loader, who came back from the RAF in 1946, had been a member of the club since 1930. Gerry learnt the game at St Bartholomew's Grammar School, Newbury, 'where the Welsh coach, Ivor Herbert, was as keen on instilling loyalty to the team and the school as he was on the skills of the game, and I have always been grateful to him for that early indoctrination', wrote Loader.

On leaving school at the age of 17½ (in 1929), Loader played a few games for the Polytechnic, but was then taken along to a Harlequin trial. Subsequently he played in the 'A', where he had the interesting experience of being told how to do his job as a hooker by a fly-half who happened to be Douglas Bader. Sixteen years later, when Loader was firmly established in the Quins' First XV, he was given a second lesson by another fly-half, this time Adrian Stoop, who had come into the changing-room after the game against Rosslyn Park to tell Loader what was wrong with his hooking.

After Loader's first contact with the Quins, he was sent up to Yorkshire, where he played for Wakefield, the club which Reg Bolton had just left. At the end of the war he decided his rugger career was over but was persuaded to continue by Alan Grimsdell, and proceeded to do so for another four seasons. In 1950, Johnny Matthews, who was then the captain of the club, suggested that Gerry should act as a 'nursemaid' for the First XV, which he did for the next eleven years.

International caps were plentiful in the late Forties and early Fifties, though some of them did not stay with the Harlequins for long. Among them was R.C.C.Thomas, a Cambridge blue who, during his rugger career, played twenty-six times for Wales, although, it must be said, mainly in his time with Swansea, of which he was the captain and mainstay. Later still, he became an outstanding sporting journalist. T.Danby, a very fast wing, did not stay with the Harlequins for long for, after being capped for England, he departed to Rugby League. M.B.Hofmeyr, who had won blues at Oxford for rugger and cricket, was principally a full-back, although also an accomplished fly-half. Although a South African by birth, he played three times for England in 1950.

Inevitably, it is easy to describe the achievements of a club in terms of First XV wins and international caps gained. However, we have made the point that with the Quins, winning is not the sole criterion and that their open style of play is probably their most valued characteristic. In any club there are always players who turn out week in, week out, and play as well, in the view of their contemporaries, as many, sometimes members of the Harlequin club and sometimes not, who are capped for their countries.

Any first-class club can probably point to at least one member who deserved to have become an international but did not quite make it. Often, such players played in international trials but were then passed over or were, perhaps, robbed of that accolade at the last moment by injury. Sometimes a player with dual qualifications is offered a trial by two countries. He then has to agonise over which offers the best opportunity. If he fails to win a cap subsequently, he then can spend the rest of his life deploring his own stupidity, which is how he will see it.

An interesting statistic appeared in 1949. The Quins' scrum-half Norman Fryer managed to play in both the English and the Welsh trials. Alas, he was not capped for either.

But, as we have said, it is not the stars who are necessarily the strength of the club. What keeps a club going in bad times is the strength of the hard-core regulars and players in the 'A's. Never was this more apparent than in the 1990-91 season when, in the last months of 1990, the Quins had 38 members unavailable, either from international trails or other calls, or injury. (This was when the club had eleven internationals).

But in less strenuous times the 'A's do an invaluable job of bringing on reserve players. Usually they are organised and often captained by experienced players who have lost the speed and agility to keep them in the First XV. During the Thirties, there had been a rough distinction between the 'A's: the First 'A' had a fixture list which would have extended any club, and the 'Schools A' tended to be on the lighter side, although sometimes carrying a former international or blue in his declining years. In 1949 it was felt that these categories should be formalised, and the First 'A' was given a change of name. The chosen title was 'Wanderers'. This was not an entirely original thought. Other clubs had similar names for their Second XVs. Coventry ran an Extra First, Moseley and

Harlequins XV that drew 6-6 with the Paris University Club in 1950. An unusual but genial pose.

Bristol had a 'United', Wasps had 'Vandals', and Saracens, rather imaginatively, had 'Crusaders'.

The Wanderers soon showed the benefit of the change for, although acting as the main reserve for the First XV, they were also a club within a club. An already strong fixture list was further strengthened and soon the Wanderers would go on their own Easter tours, latterly in France: often the opponents deemed they were the Harlequins' First XV, for they played accordingly.

Perhaps the Wanderers' best season ever was 1958-59 when, under the captaincy of D.A.Whiting, they played 32 matches, won 29 and lost three, scoring 620 points against 182. Most of their players had had First XV experience. Their scrum-half, J.Spencer, would later play for England against Wales. Spencer was a player who looked temptingly frail to opposing back-row forwards who visualised easily treading him into the turf, but he was both tough and agile and could give as good as he got. It is said that he could

Harlequins beat Cardiff 8-6 in the first floodlit game to be played in the south of England. It was staged at the White City Stadium, London, on 12 October 1954.

have earned more international caps, but by the mid Sixties he had wearied of the game and went off to live in France. He was said to have lived in a converted bus whilst in England, but from choice, not necessity; his hobbies were weaving and gymnastic ballet, and his girl friends were noted for their attractiveness and dress-sense. His sudden disappearance from the English Rugby Football scene was regarded as somewhat eccentric, but fortunately the Harlequins have had many members whose attituude to convention have not been entirely orthodox.

Sometimes, of course, the entire team can behave unconventionally. Martin Jackson, who was captain in 1949, recalls playing in a match against Blackheath. At that time England was still suffering from petrol rationing, so if any players had cars they would have been prohibited from using them for such private journeys. The team therefore set off on the Southern Railway (now

Network South-East), with the intention of taking a bus from the railway station to the ground. On arrival they discovered that there was a bus strike and they were faced with a tedious and time-consuming walk, which would make them late for kick-off. Jackson spotted an empty coal lorry and asked the driver for a lift. The driver duly obliged and deposited them outside the ground on time, but somewhat gritty.

Soon afterwards, following a match against Bristol, Jackson, Brooks and Matthews were being entertained, rather late, in an RAF mess. On the stroke of midnight the mess corporal announced that the bar was closed and the Harlequins and their hosts must leave. He then put the clock back an hour, as this was the night that winter-time began. He was then persuaded that the occupants of the bar had another hour of drinking time. When the clock reached midnight once more the corporal very agreeably put the clock back an hour once more. This happened several more times until the three Harlequins, by now showing the effects of a long day, caught the milk train back to London.

At the end of the 1949-50 season, Adrian Stoop resigned the presidency of the club, although there were many attempts to dissuade him from doing so. Wakefield, now Sir Wavell (and later to be Lord) took Adrian's place. 'Holly' Ward, whom we mentioned playing for the club before World War One, also resigned as treasurer, a post he had held since 1912. The position was taken over by D.B.(Denys) Gardiner, whose father had taken over the same duties in 1912. Ken Chapman resigned the secretaryship, which was then taken over by H.J.Gould. Jay then began a long and distinguished career in that vital position. As mentioned earlier, he had been a playing member since the early Thirties. He was one of those imperturbable people who seem to know everyone and everything, and remain unflappable during the heaviest work-load or acute crisis.

Membership flourished, so much so that on occasion the Quins even put out five teams. On 17 March 1950, the Quins beat Newport, who up until then had won thirty-two games in a row.

The Quins' Oxford University representative in the early 1950s was E.A.J.Ferguson, who subsequently played five times for Scotland. Ewen Fergusson was not only a first-class Rugby Footballer but brilliant in other spheres too, and after a distinguished career in the Diplomatic Service he has been Britain's Ambassador in France since 1987.

Whilst on the subject of high-flyers, we should mention that a Harlequin of pre-1939 vintage was Peter Rawlinson, later Lord

Rawlinson, whose career as a barrister and MP culminated in his being Attorney-General.

The new blood which came into the club in the early Fifties included H.C. (Hugh) Forbes, who had three English trials, and J.M.Williams and C.G.Woodruff. J.M.Williams was a Cornishman, although educated at Rugby; he won two England caps. Woodruff, who was another West Countryman, won four. Woodruff was one of those wing three-quarters who look capable of running through a steel fence. Roger Whyte remembered a sample of Woodruff's indestructibility. 'In about 1960, we were on a two-match tour in south-west France. Near the end of the game Peter Woodruff (his name was not really Peter) was carried off with a broken leg. We changed disconsolately, had a couple of drinks, and talked sadly about the 38-year-old Woody, whose long career looked over. We strolled back to our hotel and there was Woodruff, standing on a chair on the verandah waving his crutches in the air in greeting. He had the leg set in plaster, had left the hospital, walked a mile back to the hotel and was ready for a full night of Harlequin revelry. Oh boy, he suffered on the train the next day, but he was ready and eager four months later on 1 September.'

Some years earlier, Woodruff had been responsible for recruiting Roger Whyte to the Quins. Whyte, who had been taught Rugby Football by the Revd P.W.P.Brook at Clifton College (as we said earlier, Peter Brook supplied the Quins with many players) then went on to play for the Clifton Club (which he captained) and Gloucestershire. Whilst playing for the latter, he got to know Woodruff, who said that Whyte really ought to be playing for a first-class club and that it should be the Harlequins. In spite of Whyte's protests that he wished to stay loyal to Clifton, Woodruff persisted in this line of argument.

'Then,' said Whyte, 'one morning, out of the blue, a card dropped through my letter box. It said: "You have been selected to play for the Harlequin Wanderers v Cardiff Athletic on Saturday, 10 December at Cardiff Arms Park." Had it been any other opposition on any other ground, I would have said, "No". But Cardiff Arms Park. I played. The next week there was an England trial and many first-team Quins were involved so I got in the First XV v Newport. Once in I stayed there for several seasons.'

R.A.M.Whyte, 'Roger' or 'Chalky' as he was generally known, was probably the most versatile player ever to put on a Quins

Opposite: 'Excuse me. Mine, I think.'
A.A.Grimsdell secures the ball from a Richmond
player on 13 November 1954. Harlequins won 9-6.
(See page 96).

Bristol 21 Harlequins 5 in 1955. W.J.Leaver is the player passing the ball.

jersey. He played as a 'first choice' in every position on the field with the exception of scrum-half and even in that position he was selected for Gloucestershire. Spectators were astonished to see him hooking in one game and then playing full-back in the next. He was fast enough for a wing three-quarter and subtle enough to be a fly-half. He played for the First XV from 1954 to 1961 and then for the Wanderers for two seasons, sharing the captaincy wth Ricky Bartlett. Like Ricky he had no delusions of grandeur and would turn out in games which scarcely merited the title 'first-class'. Latterly, when he was a schoolmaster at Millfield, he was able to turn some promising players towards the Quins. Although never an international, he was a Barbarian.

Ian Beer, at the time of writing headmaster of Harrow, was recruited by Colonel John Wharton (capped for England while playing for the Harlequins in 1926 and 1927) when he was serving as a subaltern in the Royal Fusiliers in the BAOR. Soon afterwards he left the Army and went up to St Catharine's College, Cambridge, and won blues in 1952, 1953, and 1954. He was capped twice for

England in 1955. He recalls: 'The great men were David Brooks, Alan Grimsdell, whose place kick from a mark at the kick-off at Cardiff was the longest successful kick I have ever seen in person . . .out near the touch-line about fifteen yards back from the half-way line, Sandy Sanders, Nick Labuschagne, Tug Wilson, Vic Roberts, Phil Davies, Peter Woodruff and Denis Barker. I enjoyed it all and I only wish I had been able to play longer for the club.'

In the Fifties, David Brooks, who became the Harlequins' president in succession to Ken Chapman on 28 June 1990, was at the height of his playing career. M.L.'Micky' Grant wrote an account of David Brooks which needs no amendment:

'David Kenneth Brooks has packed more into his Rugby life than most of us could if we played until we were ninety.

'He was educated at Rutlish, where his contemporaries included R.T.Kindred and, of course, our present Prime Minister. As soon as he was old enough he volunteered for the Fleet Air Arm. This was the era of the famous Swordfish, an aircraft of somewhat ponderous design and purpose, but the hero of many an epic battle, rugged, dependable, and capable of withstanding much punishment. There are some who watching David in the twilight of his playing career, were struck by the comparison of the man and the machine he used to fly.

'In 1945 he was introduced to the Harlequins by two notable recruiting officers, Ken Chapman and Norman Steel, and rapidly established himself as a first-rate back-row forward and a staunch clubman off the field. He has been a reserve for England trials, represented London Counties and Surrey, captained the club for two successful seasons and the Wanderers for two more, and served on the Harlequin Committee continuously for fourteen years, where he has always been the official leader of the opposition. His work as Press Publicity Officer has been of inestimable value in maintaining the close and cordial relations with the Press which the Quins enjoy today. He is at present chairman of the Selection Committees of London and Surrey and a committee member of the Schools' Union on the latter two bodies. Surrey's success in the County Championship this season is in no small way attributable to David Brooks.

'Few of the Harlequins become legends in our own lifetime, but already an aura of myth is growing up around this remarkable character. His supernatural ability to talk his way out of hopelessly compromising situations is well known. Hotel managers, policemen, railway officials and communist security officers, have all in their time retired discomforted from a brush with Brooky.

Referees, of course, were child's play, except on one occasion when the Brooks charm failed to provide the Harlequins with our fair share of doubtful decisions. It was at the beginning of the 1958 season when several new laws had been introduced. In the bar after the game, Brooky approached the referee. "We were a bit puzzled by your interpretation of the new laws, sir." "What new laws?" replied the referee.

'His exploits in Romania (where the Harlequins toured in 1956) must have already passed into the folklore of that unhappy country. On one occasion he was taken to see a magnificent new sports stadium with luxurious changing-rooms and seating capacity for 100,000. The interpreter, with justifiable pride, told him the whole thing had been built in four months. Brooky stared round in puzzled, apparently sympathetic, innocence. "What held you up?" he asked.

'Romania is a country where it is the funeral custom for the deceased to be carried fully dressed to his final resting place. On one of their journeys between matches, the Harlequins met such a procession and were distinctly unnerved to observe that the dead man looked considerably fitter than the Harlequins. Romanian hospitality the previous evening had been very generous.

'David Brooks managed the 1965 Harlequin tour to South Africa: it is believed we were the first club to tour that country. The experience stood him in good stead when he was appointed manager of the British Lions tour of South Africa in 1968.

'He was president of the Surrey Rugby Football Union from 1971 to 1973; he had played for Surrey from 1945-52, being captain for the last three years of that time. He was also president of the London Rugby Football Union, the only Harlequin to hold that post. He was president of the Rugby Football Union for the season 1981-82.

'Anyone seeing this list of Brooky's high-level appointments might conclude he must by now be rather a pompous fellow. They would be quite wrong: he is just the opposite.'

We started this description of David Brooks in his playing days in the Fifties. To these we must now return.

A very useful recruit in 1950 was A.E.'Albert' Agar, who came to the Harlequins from Lloyds Bank. He was usually a centre, although he could play fly-half. Agar, who played seven times for England, was a member of the London Counties which accomplished the historic feat of beating the 1951 Springboks touring team by 11-9. This performance was all the more remarkable for the fact that the Springboks won all their other twenty-six

Sandy Sanders powers through the Cardiff pack in December 1955.

matches in England, Scotland, Ireland and Wales. In addition to Agar, the Quins had Johnny Matthews, Hugh Forbes and Alan Grimsdell. Grimsdell was a prodigious kicker, credited more than once with eighty-yard place kicking and on this occasion kicked a vital penalty goal. The boots he wore in this match are now on view in the Rugby Football Museum at Twickenham.

Alan and his brother W.R. 'Billy' were the sons of a famous soccer player, Arthur Grimsdell, a wing-half for Tottenham Hotspur and England (for which he won six caps). He is generally rated as having been one of the best half-backs in the history of Association Football, if not the best. Although slight in build,

Very cheerful. An informal picture of the Quins. G.G.Woodruff is seated extreme left. M.L.Grant is seated second from right.

he too had a prodigious kick, which goalkeepers dreaded. In temperament he was unassuming and imperturbable. As with the Chapman family, the boys went to a rugger playing school, although when in the Services, they played both games at every opportunity. Alan Grimsdell had learnt his rugger at Watford Grammar School and Berkhamsted. Apart from playing for the Quins, he was also in the Middlesex team from 1949-53, had an England trial in 1951 and was travelling reserve for England in the 1951-52 season. He was chairman of the Buckinghamshire RFU from 1960-81, was honorary treasurer of the RFU from 1981 to 1984 and was president of the RFU from 1986 to 1987. There can be few people who have put more back into the game than Alan has.

After Alan Grimsdell had completed his playing days in the First XV, and had one or two England trials, he captained the Wanderers. He also played for Buckinghamshire, which at that time was one of the leading counties and came near to winning the Championship.

A very welcome arrival in 1950 was V.G.(Vic) Roberts from

Cornwall, where he had been playing for Penryn and had already won several of the England caps he eventually achieved. As his international career shows, he was a very skilled and well-organised wing-forward. In those days forwards could still stand as close to each other as they wished in the line-out and often purposely trod on each other's feet in doing so, and the only way of getting a clean ball to one's three-quarters was to throw a long ball to a safe catcher such as Vic Roberts, who would then set off like a streak of light before transferring the ball to the fly-half. A throw-in which landed in the centre of the line-out might or might not be caught cleanly and passed, or heeled back. Occasionally the less intelligent forwards would try to knock the ball back to the scrum-half, to whom it would arrive in company with a couple of the opposition forwards who (probably offside) had burst through. 'Knocking back' was discouraged, although not entirely eliminated, because it tended to raise the mortality rate among scrum-halves. Wing-forwards, although cursed generally by the Press, spectators and fellow-players alike, were usually blamed for sins they had not committed, principally that of destroying open football. In fact, wing-forwards like Vic Roberts often assisted passing movements by being on hand to take a reverse pass, join in the three-quarter line or snap up a loose ball.

Another brilliant wing-forward was D.S.'Tug' Wilson, who joined the Harlequins from the Metropolitan Police and went on to win eight caps in the Fifties. 'Tug' Wilson served in one of the undercover branches of the police and while doing so contrived to be remarkably inconspicuous. At Twickenham and elsewhere his presence was unmistakeable.

The Fifties also saw the arrival of W.P.C.Davies, who was soon well on his way to winning eleven England caps. Phil Davies was a fair-haired, bulky three-quarter with a devastating break-through. He was a product of Denstone College and was noted for his amiability. However, fellow players did not fail to observe that a pass from Davies was likely to be at your feet or over your head and would have given Adrian Stoop great mental pain. Adrian invariably watched matches from behind the goalposts in the North Stand because he felt that this was the best point from which to judge the three-quarters.

Phil Davies was up at Cambridge in the early Fifties, where he knew Ricky and John Bartlett and Micky Grant. He could run quite fast, but not fast enough to get a running blue. Although he played once or twice for the University XV, he did not get a Rugby blue either. In fact, if he had not played in the Quins

In 1956 the Harlequins beat a German XV 26-8 at Twickenham. They were the first German touring side to visit Britain. In this photograph R.M.Bartlett of the Quins tackles P.Bach.

trials in 1951 he might not have had a career in first-class rugger at all. As it was, he turned out at fly-half and on the strength of his play in that position was, rather surprisingly, chosen for the First XV at full-back the following Saturday. In successive weeks he played at wing, centre, and fly-half. In January 1958, when he had just taken up the headmastership of Denstone Preparatory School, he received his last international cap and this gave the club the unique distinction of having as a member the only headmaster currently playing international rugger.

Earlier he had been in the 1955 British Lions tour of South Africa. This tour had been the most successful of the century and ended in a victory for the Lions in the first international by 23-22 on what, coincidentally, was Phil Davies' birthday. The South Africans scored a try in the closing minutes and hoped to secure victory by one point by converting. The kick failed but the ball was caught by Davies who was able to retain it.

Phil Davies recalls: 'Memories of the Quins Rugby of the Fifties are full of joy, the variety of background, from a barrister (Dennis Barker) to a paddle-steamer engineer (Roger Whyte, as versatile in his profession as he was in his play), the camaraderie, the good humour (the front row wearing perfume to persuade West Country opposition that they were London softies), and the intense commitment under Johnny Matthews, David Brooks and Ricky Bartlett, and for me at least the intensity of training and preparation; if only the Quins had had the modern dietary regimes and housekeeping money. Gradually during this time, the forwards became much fitter and more mobile, the late Peter Robbins, of Oxford and Coventry, showing how to get from set positions and amongst the opposition backs for second phase. The only really fit sides were touring or at Oxford, or, more probably, Cambridge. Life became more difficult if one had to beat opposition centres, always possible, but the back row as well.

'Most remembered is Ricky Bartlett, laid back, thoughtful and with his farming-gnarled, utterly safe hands, deadly kicks to Peter Woodruff at the corner and his beautifully timed passes to inside centre. never a bad one. Once in 1957 he saved my reputation against France. I was on the rampage and having beaten the centre reached the French full-back, only for my pass putting Peter Jackson away to be intercepted. Ricky, covering, cut him off and as I puffed back said quietly, "Don't do that again, Phil."

'The game has become interesting again after the doldrums of the late Seventies and early Eighties. So much is now neater, tidier and more skilful as forward fitness is now phenomenal. The advent of floodlighting has made proper coaching and training possible and the standard of co-ordination, formerly only met on tour or at university, are now a facet of even junior clubs. Having played until I was forty-nine, and winning a local junior club medal at the age of forty-four, I would still like to play in today's conditions

The date is 28 September 1957 and the Harlequins beat Leicester 19-6. R.A.M.Whyte tackles D.W.Matthews (Leicester).

but doubt if I would have made much progress, not being willing to play three times a week except on rare occasions. If I did I would practise three techniques for the modern game:

One: My controlled jiggle of the ball, which counted as a knock-on in my day but is now the best of dummies.

Two: Remain standing rather than going to ground.

100

Action against Richmond at the White City in 1958. R.Whyte is on the left. R.W.D.Marques is to the right. Are they Quins hands on the ball?

Three: Go into the opposition at two-thirds speed and look for support as I did so.

Four: Improve my dive on to the loose ball.'

One's comment on this is that it would not be nearly as

The Quins in action against St Mary's Hospital in 1958 and the Harlequin ballet gives a performance. In air is John Hancock; on the ground (left) is Grahame Murray; Howard Hoare is number-nine.

entertaining to watch as the way Phil Davies used to play when he went through the centre like a bullet. Although he feels that modern play is probably faster all round than it was in his day, it seems to be over-influenced by heavy packs of forwards building up pressure on the opposition, who then give away penalties. He would prefer, as we all would, to see more 'second phase' running.

J.D.Currie passing when tackled by a Leicester player at Twickenham in 1959. Note the sparse number of spectators in the stand.

The only experts at this seem to be the French, although the Scots are developing it too!

Phil Davies also played soccer, hockey and cricket. Although he was an above-average runner, he preferred running against people rather than against the clock. But his warmest memories are of his days with the Quins: 'The humour, the kindness, the dedication of players and especially committeemen: Gerry Loader, Howell Thomas, Jay Gould, Ken Chapman.'

Before retiring from schoolmastering he ran the Cheltenham College Junior School for twenty-two years. He is now involved

Quins v Oxford University at Twickenham in 1959. R.W.D.Marques gets possession of the ball.

with Conservatives, and builds kit cars and classic motor cycles, as well as working with the disabled and the Cheshire Homes.

Meanwhile, in the Fifties the Wanderers and the 'A's were going from strength to strength. Both won the majority of their matches. One of the 'A's was captained by Peter Stoop, son of F.M. and nephew of Adrian. Much of the success of the Wanderers and 'A' teams was now due to the fact that former First XV players, feeling that *anno domini* was catching up, had decided to put off their final retirement by playing in the lesser teams where they thought the pace would be less exhausting. This did not always seem to be the case, as the opposition usually seemed determined to prove it was good enough for a First XV fixture.

The number of players who were selected for trials in 1952 may well be a record for any club. They were D.A.Barker, H.C.Forbes, J.M.Williams, L.D.Ashcroft, V.G.Roberts, J.R.C.Matthews, H.G.Greatwood, A.E.Agar, N.Labuschagne, W.P.C.Davies,

D.S.Wilson, J.Greenwood, E.A.J.Ferguson and R.C.C.Thomas, in other words, nearly a whole XV. Many of them went on to win international caps, notably J.M.Williams, V.G.Roberts, J.R.C.Matthews, A.E.Agar, N.Labuschagne, W.P.C.Davies, D.S.Wilson, E.A.J.Fergusson and J.Greenwood. Small wonder that with this reservoir of talent, the Quins had great success in seven-a-side competitons. Nick Labuschagne, who was a student at Guy's Hospital, played five times for England before returning to South Africa. He is now president of the Natal RFU, which in 1991 won the Currie Cup. He appeared at the Stoop on 23 February 1991, when Ken Chapman's portrait was unveiled and the Quins beat Rosslyn Park in the Pilkington Cup quarter-finals. He was as cheerful, unassuming and friendly as ever.

From the Fifties to the Sixties

IT IS impossible to tell who was the fastest wing three-quarter ever to play for the Harlequins but many people think it may have been J.R.C.Young, who was an England sprinter (like A.G.Butler) even before he joined the club. A product of Bishop Vesey's Grammar School, Birmingham, and Oxford, John Young had won blues for rugger and athletics and then played for Moseley. He toured Australia and New Zealand with the British Lions in 1959. His play had much more to it than sheer speed, as those whom he either outwitted, or tackled, would readily testify. By profession he was a solicitor. Eventually he won nine caps.

The Marques-Currie partnership was also functioning very efficiently at this time. R.W.D.Marques was a 6ft 5in second-row forward, weighing close on 16st. After Tonbridge, Cambridge and the Army (National Service in the Royal Engineers), he toured Canada and South Africa with the Barbarians, and Australia and New Zealand with the British Lions. In all, he was capped twenty-three times. By profession David Marques was a civil engineer.

The other half of the partnership was J.D.Currie. John Currie was two inches shorter and a stone lighter than Marques. When still at Bristol Grammar School he had been picked to play for Gloucestershire: later he chose to throw in his lot with Somerset, for whom he played both rugger and cricket. He had been at Oxford at the same time as Marques had been at Cambridge; the two had therefore played four university matches against each other. Eventually he won twenty-five England caps.

Nicknamed 'Muscles', Currie was one of those rare people who refuse to be 'needled', however great the provocation. As we all know only too well, there have always been attempts to provoke a star of the other side into retaliatory action which may make him fall foul of the referee, but any evildoer who thought of trying this sort of thing on John Currie would have been wasting his time.

The Wanderers v Old Belvedere in 1959 (see page 87). This was probably the most successful of all Wanderers teams. The captain is D.A.Whiting. J.Spencer, the England scrum-half, is in front (right).

From 1980 to 1988, John Currie was chairman of the Harlequins. From 1986 to 1988 he was an England selector. Typical of the man was the reply he made to his old friend, John Mason, the *Daily Telegraph* Rugby correspondent. Asked why he had been fairly inactive in some of the line-outs in front of the West Stand during an England trial, he answered: "I only jump on the other side of the field. Then the selectors can see the number on my jersey when I go up."

The year 1962 saw the arrival of J.G.Willcox in the England team. John Willcox was a full-back whom the Press used to describe as 'the man who knows no fear'. His Rugby Football career had developed through Sandhurst, the Army, Harlequins, Oxford and Lancashire. When winning his first rugger blue in 1959, he also won the match for Oxford by kicking four penalty goals. He was also a boxing blue. Eventually he won seven caps and would undoubtedly have won more had it not been for injury. After leaving Oxford he became a schoolmaster at Ampleforth where, year after

Action from games against Leicester. Above: in 1960, Grahame Murray is in possession. Opposite page: in 1961, Marques becomes airborne.

year, he has produced match-winning teams at both fifteen and seven-a-side.

Although John Willcox was a remarkably safe full-back under the high ball, he did not discover, until he went on tour in South Africa in 1962, that his eyesight was defective and he needed contact lenses. The idea of playing first-class rugger with contact lenses was still something of a novelty in those days; subsequently it was not uncommon to see players lose a lens and be assisted by both teams to find it again in the churned up grass and mud.

John was never sure when people wanted to meet him, whether it was for himself or for the fact that he was Sheila Willcox's brother. She won the Three-Day Event at Badminton in 1956, 1957 and 1958, and was European Champion in 1957 and 1959 in Turin and Copenhagen: in those days girls were not allowed to ride in the Olympics.

John Willcox recalled a tour in France when after the game they were being entertained in some style. Ricky Bartlett was sitting in the place of honour next to the president of the French club and the hospitality had been almost too lavish. Some misguided person then set off a thunderflash, which brought down the glass-enclosed light near to where Bartlett and the president were sitting. It crashed on to the table and shattered, taking the top of Bartlett's wine glass with it. 'Ricky's glass was broken but he still held the

R.A.M Whyte and M.L.Grant pictured at the White City, where Harlequins played a number of matches in the 1950s whilst waiting for the Stoop Ground.

stem and carried on with what he was saying with no change of voice or expression. A remarkable performance, considering it could have killed him.'

Willcox continued playing for the Quins until 1965 but as he had then joined the staff at Ampleforth he played for Headingley for a year. He stopped playing in 1967.

M.L.Grant was one of the club's livelier backs in the 1950 and 1965 periods. Micky Grant, who was a medium size, red-haired, three-quarter, had been at Cambridge for three years without getting a blue but then followed in the footsteps of other non-blues by getting international caps. More remarkably, he was selected for his first cap for Scotland when playing for the Wanderers. It was against France in 1955, a considerable baptism of fire. Of Grant's four caps, three were against France, the other was against Wales. Fate could have been kinder to him. Micky's social qualities were of the type which are known as 'irrepressible'.

D.L.'Sandy' Sanders came to the club in 1953, played for England five times in 1954 and four more in 1956. Subsequently he has been an England selector and honorary treasurer and president of the RFU. He was honorary manager of the England team which toured Fiji and New Zealand in 1973. It beat Fiji 13-12 and the All Blacks by 16-12.

May 1960 saw the launch of that invaluable club magazine *Harlequinade.* It was edited by Howell Thomas; Reggie Kindred looked after production and photographs, Micky Grant dealt with correspondence, articles and club news and R.S.'Ray' Relf was responsible for club records, Press comment and announcements. It opened with a message from Lord Wakefield in which he emphasised that the Harlequins was a social as well as a Rugby Football club, and that the social side, with its cricket, golf, dinners, dances, and even a game of soccer now and again, makes a vital contribution to the unity of the Harlequins.

He added a cautionary note:

There is one thing to which I would like to draw your attention.

Whenever I see a penalty-kick awarded against the club I am ashamed. It means that a Harlequin player has been fouling or cheating, and if that is the case then the sooner he stops playing Rugby Football the better. Or it means that the player is ignorant of the laws of the game and that, for a Harlequin, is no excuse at all.

What a splendid thing it would be for their club and for Rugby football if the Quins could get the reputation of winning their matches without having penalty-kicks given against us.

Members with long memories read these wise words thoughtfully, recalling that, in his playing days, Wakers was not unfamiliar with some of the transgressions he deplored.

Although the First XV had been bristling with talent in the 1959 season — J.G.Willcox, J.J.McPartlin, G.C.Murray, J.S.M.Scott, R.M.Bartlett, J.D.Currie and R.A.M.Whyte in particular — the results had been inconsistent and caused David Marques to deliver a mild rocket under 'Captain's Comments'.

Admittedly, in some of the games the Quins had been weakened by the loss of members to international or trial games, but even when they had been at full strength, their performance was sometimes 'apathetic'. David Marques announced that in the following season, three First XV games would be played at Teddington instead of at the White City, but before that happened a lot of improvements would need to be made to the accommodation at Teddington, which had never been good and was now nearly derelict. He stressed that the labour would have to come from volunteers in the summer. He added that the club needed more training sessions and that these would happen in the middle of August.

Thirty-one years later the Quins see that players now tend to remain in training through most of the summer and may well play, too, on overseas tours. Marques was the right man to put some fire into the belly of the club. According to Terry O'Connor, he was the son of an Australian who came to Britain after fighting in World War One, married a Llanelli girl, the daughter of a Welsh headmaster, and played for Blackheath and London Welsh when those teams visited the Principality.

Harlequinade brought to the notice of members many aspects of the club which previously were little known. One was the cricket side. It included a report on a tour in Norfolk which in theory was a disaster but in practice was hilarious. Based on North Wootton, it had fixtures with West Norfolk Cricket Club on the Saturday and with Castle Rising on the Sunday. In the event, there was continuous rain from Friday night until Monday morning and not a ball was bowled. However, the Red Cat Hotel, in which they were staying, rose to the occasion and laid on entertainment including top-level dance music. The lack of cricket soon became the least of their worries.

The Editor took the opportunity to point out that more 'spotters' were needed to watch the 'A' teams, some of whose members would soon, no doubt, be welcome in the First XV. A number of promising 'A' team players, were mentioned by name and the predictions proved correct. But it did not alter the fact that more of the older, retired players were required for the rewarding and pleasant duty of spotting.

In the following issue, Marques' comments struck a sterner, but necessary, note. He re-emphasised the need to train, but also stressed that players should take part in all club activities, not just turn up, play a game, have a bath and slope off immediately. He made the point which unfortunately had to be made decade after decade. Clubs prosper because members put back into the game as much as, or more than, they got out of it.

For the first time the Quins saw in print what many Harlequins must have heard verbally, although not necessarily in the same words or as neatly and gently expressed. It was the view of the long-suffering wife . . .and was entitled 'Bird's Eye View'.

I realise of course that anything I say is bound to be regarded as sacrilege by any right-thinking male, but the full extent of my redundancy has only just struck me. Let's face it: no man really cares about how his wife views the rugger months and every wife knows as much as I do about them. They are all preparing to smile acidly at husbands who attempt to jolly them along with a 'but it's only one afternoon a week'.

J.D.Currie in possession against St Mary's Hospital at Twickenham in 1958.

Somehow I'm always made to look dim when I start adding up Monday committee meetings, Thursday training (an institution not above suspicion I feel) and Sunday games. If there is no Sunday game there is liable to be a day of reckoning, either steeped in alcoholic gloom or spent contemplating sundry minute but apparently excruciating cuts and bruises; what's more each one has a story attached.

Then there are the difficulties of the Saturday wardrobe. If you vote for comfort and sally forth in slacks, boots and three layers of nondescript 'woollies', you're likely to feel fine all the afternoon, even to the extent of a few catty laughs at the expense of the girl in front who is obviously frozen in her suit and who keeps sinking into the mud and emerging each *time with more and more leather scraped from the back of her high heels.*

Around seven o'clock, however, when you are convinced that you have been at Teddington (or the Stoop) since last Saturday, some female who has just arrived and who has evidently put in a useful afternoon at home doing her nails and putting herself into a little black dress, suggests that everyone should move on up to town for a meal. With this situation ever likely to hit you, I find that a complete change of clothing is essential for peace of mind. And what does it matter if your kit does take up more room in the back of the car than his does?

Now, before I'm condemned as not having the right attitude, and not deserving to have a fine, upright, rugger-playing husband, I must tell you about my most recent attempt at being a good 'you just go along and enjoy yourself' type of wife. I was the lone girl in a group, discussing a forthcoming tour. On being asked the arch, and inevitable, 'and are you going to let him go?' I answered, 'Of course', and went on to elaborate to the effect that I thought the girls who were thinking of going along should be discouraged. At which innocent (if slightly treacherous) remark I was rounded on by every man within earshot and accused of making shameful plans of my own for that weekend . . .which is obviously the answer to the rugger season.

Be that as it may, no one doubts that the club would not have lasted for 125 years unless it had had the unstinted support of ladies like the above who, back in Victoria's reign cheered on the touch-line where their crinolines brushed the mud, and administered first aid with a sponge filled with brandy.

More recently they have served teas and drinks, sold tickets and programmes, and generally, though unobtrusively, created order where chaos of all types had formerly reigned. Nowadays, and long overdue, they can become members in their own right.

In spite of Marques' exhortations the Sixties began disastrously. The decade is, of course, well known as the time when everything began to go to the dogs, but one hardly expected the Harlequin Football Club to be swept along on the tide of the decline.

The Quins did, however, manage to beat the Wolfhounds (the Irish Barbarians) in the Adrian Stoop Memorial Match on 10 September (by one point), in a match that was noteworthy for

Opposite: Adrian Stoop in later years but as enthusiastic as ever. He died in 1957, aged 74. This portrait is by D.Q.Fildes.

the fact that Grahame Murray, the Quins' prop forward, scored a try in the corner after handing off several determined Irishmen on his way there. Front-row forwards are not normally seen understudying to be wing three-quarters, particularly if they are as large as Grahame Murray. Otherwise the only bit of good news was that Sir Bernard Waley-Cohen, a good Harlequin, had been elected Lord Mayor of London.

Four Harlequin captains who all became presidents of the Rugby Football Union (from left to right): V.H.Cartwright, A.D.Stoop, J.E.Greenwood, W.W.Wakefield.

For Quins' matches in the very early days of the club they were able to rely on the services of W.E.Titchener to give a faithful, if sometimes a little fanciful, report in *The Field*.

In the Sixties this tradition was revived when Hylton Cleaver, another old member and a respected journalist, also began writing a page of Rugby Football news also in *The Field*.

Not surprisingly, the fortunes of the Harlequins were not neglected. Hylton's own career had been rather like that of one of the characters in the enormously popular boys' school stories he used to write. When he had been at St Paul's he was at first forbidden to play games because of acute asthma. His circulation was so bad that his nose earned him the nickname of 'Raspberry Tip'. When he was allowed to play rugger later he was so short-

At Richmond in 1959, R.A.M.Whyte and D.J.Pack pictured as the ball goes loose.

sighted that he scored what he thought was his first try on his opponents' 25 (22 metre) line.

However, by determination he improved, eventually played for Middlesex, rowed in the Grand Challenge Cup at Henley and was vice-captain of Belsize Boxing Club for eight years. He also won an MC in World War One. Not a bad sample of Harlequin.

Wakelam was, of course, a journalist, and so was Howard Marshall, but it is less well known that Terry O'Connor, of the *Daily Mail* has also worn the Harlequin jersey. Terry commented that few clubs command such loyalty from their members and, in particular, commended Roger Whyte who, he felt, would have received an England cap if he had stayed in the front-row and not allowed himself to be used as a general utility man. One doubts, however, whether Roger lost much sleep over that.

Another piece of 'history repeating itself' occurred in 1961. R.J.'Dick' Leonard, a Cambridge blue and England trialist, was serving in the Army in Germany. He wrote: 'Things are pretty quiet over here, except for BAOR games, of which the Quins have led one this season at Frankfurt. Greg Read and David Mallam were playing, so the club was well represented. After the Quins had beaten the Frankfurt Club (the 1880 Club) 36-9, they challenged us to a series of beer-drinking races, as they considered themselves pretty good at that. But they never stood a chance, and the Quins beat them three times on the trot, at which stage they gave up, while the Quins were quite prepared to go on.'

But this time no one was elected 'Beer King of Germany'.

Another of the Quins' Army members renewed contact in 1961. This was Nick Raffle, a former Cambridge blue, who had been playing for Accra in Ghana. Raffle forecast that Ghana would soon be producing good rugger players. How right he was.

Although the Sixties had begun rather shakily, there were signs of a better future. The Colts, a very useful source of recruits, were thriving under the guidance of Sandy Sanders. Teddington, which had been refurbished, was now popular as a social centre in which all teams would occasionally congregate, a golfing society was launched and disclosed some unexpected talent, the First XV was moderately successful and all the other teams were apparently unbeatable. Many of the Quins' 1991 playing members were not even born in the early Sixties, but have benefited from the changes and improvements made at that time.

Among the newcomers were J.E.(Johnny) Williams, C.P.(Colin) Simpson, G.(Graham) McElwee, and J.(Jeremy) Taylor. Johnny Williams had been playing scrum-half for the Old Millhillians, Middlesex, and England. He already had seven England caps and would win another in 1963. He had a pass of electrifying speed.

Colin Simpson was in the Army and would have the unique distinction of being capped for England in 1965 whilst a cadet at the Royal Military Academy, Sandhurst. He was a large, strong-running wing three-quarter. Jimmy Taylor was a centre who had been spotted by Roger Whyte in the West Country. Graham McElwee came from further afield, New Zealand, in fact. He was a prop forward, built on classic New Zealand lines.

The season 1961-62 was such a successful one for the Wanderers and the 'A' that the question of running two First XVs was seriously considered. The core of the problem was that the Wanderers were too strong for most of the teams they played. However, few clubs which rated themselves as first-class were prepared to put their first team against the Wanderers, considering that to play the Harlequin Second XV was below their dignity, whatever the result might be. But, even if the Quins ran two First XVs, there would be plenty of eagle-eyed opponents suspecting that they had been fobbed off with the one which would otherwise have been the Wanderers.

There might be awkward problems of administration too. It was suggested that the Quins should increase the number of midweek matches and by that give more Wanderers a taste of First XV football. However, midweek fixtures were liable to clash with county games, not to mention their interference with the tedious business of earning a living. A suggestion was made that the titles First, Wanderers, and 'A' should be abolished and every team should just be Harlequins. No solution has been found to this dilemma and the club still continues to lose highly promising players to other clubs when they feel their hold on a regular first-team place with the Quins slipping.

The other side of the coin is that, while the club maintains a very high standard of play, they attract members from other clubs who feel that playing for the Quins would either sharpen up their prospects of an international cap, or simply be more fun. So perhaps what the Harlequins lose on the roundabouts they gain on the swings.

Looking at a fixture card at random gives an interesting insight on who was shouldering the administrative burden in any given year. In 1962, W.W.Wakefield was president, David Brooks was chairman, Colin Payne was captain, and Derek Whiting was secretary (assisted by P.C.Forbes). H.J.Gould was fixtures secretary, assisted by H.G.Thomas. J.S.M.Scott was fifty per cent of the finance committee (the other fifty per cent was R.W.D.Marques) but Scott was also involved with 'social activities' and Colts. Howell Thomas was also editor of *Harlequinade*; ten years earlier he had been team secretary for the Wanderers and the 'A' XVs, and for many years before that fixtures secretary for the Wanderers and 'A' XVs. Thirty years later, in 1991, he is a vice-president and is still editing *Harlequinade*.

In 1962 the Quins had their first secretary of the Rugby Football Union who was Robin Prescott. Later they would have others and, of course, the Harlequin FC has had more presidents than any other club. Being secretary of the RFU is a fairly hot seat, for whatever goes wrong is blamed on to the secretary and every secretary is well aware of Murphy's Law: 'If anything can go wrong it will go wrong'.

The trials at the beginning of the 1962-63 season produced an interesting comment in *Harlequinade*:

> *There was an outstanding brilliance in the three games played, but a number of younger players gave an impression*

of increased maturity. Both centres in the senior side, Gibbs and Lloyd, ran well, a happy augury, for it is here the Quins seem in greatest need. A schoolboy, Hiller, made a fine impression at full-back, and there appeared any number of industrious back-row forwards.

Wise words. J.D.Gibbs was the son of the industrious J.C.Gibbs, and would soon be in the First XV. R.H.Lloyd would play for England five times before the end of the decade, and R.B.Hiller would later become so firmly established as the England full-back that no one else got a look in for twenty matches.

The second comment in *Harlequinade* ran as follows:

'The following appeared recently in the *Evening Standard* Londoner's Diary:

Bob Waller is a husky giant whose 6ft 2in and 15½st lends crushing weight as a second-row forward in the Harlequin pack. What's the line of this solid piece of he-man?

Nobody would ever guess him to be a maker of women's hats in the family business at Luton, where he personally adds the finishing touch of ribbons, bows or feathers that adorns his models.'

The writer of the 'Londoner's Diary' should not have been surprised. All Harlequins have a well-developed touch of artistry, although usually it is displayed in tactical moves on the field of play.

The year 1963 showed a steady improvement as the season got into its stride. Coincidentally, Geoff Butler was president of the RFU in a year when John Young, another England sprinter, was playing on the wing. The international Joe McPartlin and the future one, Bob Lloyd, were the centres and the other backs were of much the same standard. John Willcox was his usual rock-steady self at full-back. There were some heavy guns up front. Grahame Murray and David Wrench were on either side of the front row and J.L. 'Ballgetter' Bazalgette was hooker. In the second row were Colin Payne and David Marques and behind them were Marriot, Todman and Mallet. Llanelly and Leicester were early victims. Hiller appeared at full-back in October 1963 and there was no shortage of reserves if any of them were not available.

This was the first season in which the Quins had broken with a tradition which went back to the founding of the club: the Quins admitted some non-playing members. Previously all Quins had to be players, and players of certain standard of efficiency at that. Nevertheless, facts had to be faced, particularly financial ones, and in the days of soaring costs the Quins simply did not have enough revenue.

It would have been ridiculous to push the subscription up to a point at which no one could afford to pay or play and there is a limit to what can be raised from dances, raffles, etc. In fact, necessity was soon shown to have been a virtue, for their non-playing members threw themselves into the task of being worthy Harlequins with such vigour that the Quins became a more efficient club all round.

Notable among their non-playing members was (and is) Pat Meaney (now Sir Patrick), who was managing director of Thomas Tilling Limited and later director of Cable & Wireless and ICI. He is also chairman of the Rank Organisation, and of Mecca Leisure, and director and deputy chairman of Midland Bank. Meaney soon identified the area where the Quins needed to be jollied along a bit and nobody who saw him in action was surprised later by his great success in the business world.

The date 16 November 1963 is a historic one in the club's history, for it was on that day that the Quins moved into the new Stoop Memorial ground at Craneford Way. Negotiations for their move from Teddington to this new site had been begun in 1960. It now proved an excellent pitch, a fine clubhouse with stand accommodation for 600 spectators and good parking facilities. A second pitch was being prepared. In the event the running track was a dubious asset, for it made the distance from the stand to the pitch unduly wide. In 1990 it was covered in and the pitch brought correspondingly nearer to the stand, making the Stoop look more like a Rugby Football ground than an athletic track of which the centre was used for other purposes.

As the First XV was playing Oxford at Twickenham on that day, the Quins arranged a game between their veterans and a combined veterans XV from Richmond and London Scottish.

There was much good-humoured banter in the dressing-rooms before the match, as such ancient warriors as A.A.Grimsdell, P.D.Strang and N.Gibbs unearthed ancient cracking boots and shorts, yellow with age, from their bags. George Plumtree thought fit to celebrate the occasion by buying a brand new pair of Cotton Oxfords, and the daddy of us all, Peter Brook, a stripling of 55 who captained the side, insisted on wearing his old jersey, thereby producing a powerful aroma of mothballs to mingle with the smell of wintergreen and other lotions being hopefully applied to check the years.

G.V.Carey, who had kicked-off in the first match at Twickenham in 1909, did so on this occasion too. In the event the veterans all played with astonishing skill and vigour and the match ended in a draw.

Beneficial though this move to the Stoop was, there were inevitable problems, of which the largest was making it pay its way. A sub-committee was formed to deal with the administrative problems created by their new and much-loved baby.

D.A.Whiting was the first chairman and P.M.Meaney vice-chairman. However, it was arranged that within a short time Whiting would be released from his duties (and continue as an ex-officio member) and Meaney take his place. P.C.Forbes would be secretary. Other members of this sub-committee would be R.L.Hudson, R.S.Relf, W.B.Shires, R.F.Crichton, J.Seldon, R.Carter, R.J.J.Pollock and R.E.Wright, all having their special responsibilities.

After the builders had left the Stoop it presented a somewhat bleak scene. John Scott decided its appearance would be improved by the presence of a few trees and proceeded to provide them and plant them himself. Inevitably some were destroyed by vandals, but were replaced. The result is that the Stoop is now an attractive ground and as the years pass will be more so.

As an example of the wide range of the Quins commitments, we can summarise those of the 1962-63 season.

John Willcox played for England and the Barbarians. Five other Quins had England trials (their turns would come later). Twelve Quins played for Surrey, five for Middlesex, two for Herts, one for the Eastern Counties, one for Somerset, one for Warwickshire, one for Cheshire, two for Lancashire, one for Durham, one for Kent and one for Leinster. J.J.McPartlin captained Oxford University and N.Silk was the captain-elect. K.J.H.Mallet played for the RAF and M.Handfield-Jones and C.P.Simpson for the Army. Handfield-Jones was a highly promising centre who would undoubtedly have been in the running for an England cap but was soon afterwards killed by a bomb in Aden.

As the Quins moved into the Stoop, on the very doorstep of Twickenham, it was appropriate to remind ourselves that this did not weaken, but probably strengthened, their link with the great Mecca of Rugby Football (at which the Quins are still entitled to play thirteen times a year, although this is now impossible). Their new premises would provide a congenial place for meeting old friends, for Twickenham, with up to 60,000 attending an international match, was scarcely the place for calmly recalling old times. In some ways the scrum around the bars made Twickenham more like a re-run of earlier playing experiences.

The August 1963 issue of *Harlequinade* published a letter from J.C.Gibbs which contained a suggestion that, if implemented, could have a beneficial effect on the game nearly thirty years later. His proposal concerned the drop-kick:

> *The drop-kick is peculiar to rugger and it is a most difficult kick to direct with any accuracy whether the kicker is under pressure or not. Most players can punt; few players can drop-kick. A punt is generally a 'coarse' sort of action; a drop-kick is more graceful. When a ball is punted it seems to be aware that it has been treated as though it were of no consequence: where a ball is drop-kicked it clearly realises that it has been treated with respect as it soars into the air.*
>
> *Therefore, why not consider doing away with time-wasting place-kicks and penalty-kicks and let all kicks (perhaps with the exception of kicks from the 'mark' be by drop-kicking. Let all penalty-kicks be drop-kicks and last, but not least, let all kicks to touch be drop-kicks.*

The proposal opened up a fascinating prospect but was too revolutionary to be accepted officially. At the time the letter was published there was great dissastisfaction with the way games were often ruined by fly-halves kicking monotonously to touch to gain ground rather than passing the ball to their three-quarters. Eventually this practice was stopped by the current rule, which comes close to the practice in Rugby League, of only being allowed to kick direct into touch from inside one's own twenty-two. Beyond that, the ball must, of course, roll into touch. There has also grown up the practice of short-tapped penalties; this was not unknown in the old days either, but not used so much.

The Quins were not sorry to see the rule change over touch-kicking, for although it was against their principles to gain ground by long touch-kicks, it was often used against them. Many international matches were spoilt by endless, dreary long-range kicks into touch and spectators at Twickenham or Cardiff or Murrayfield, though not so much in Dublin or Paris, would see three-quarters of proved genius kept completely starved of the ball. Gibbs' drop-kick rule would have immediately checked the fly-halves who worked their way up the touch line with kicks while their three-quarters froze to death, mentally as well as physically.

Bob Read and Vic Marriot went on the England tour of Australia and New Zealand, during which Vic Marriot played in the two

Test Matches against New Zealand. The following year he gained another international cap against Australia.

Rugby Football, or a version of it, is now played in most countries in the world. Some Harlequins will remember playing in Malaya, when the temperature was over ninety degrees and when the first pint after the game seemed to disappear even before it had touched the drinker's lips. Others will remember playing in Spain on ground like concrete, bare of grass but marked out for other types of game: soccer, hockey, or even more exotic pastimes. One of these might still be occupying the pitch when the Quins arrived for the advertised kick-off.

In 1963, Pat Cleaver added another dimension by refereeing a game between Sweden and Denmark. It was a totally unexpected privilege. Having arrived in Copenhagen, where he met the president of the Danish Rugby Union, he was informed that Denmark would be playing Sweden the following Sunday and if no neutral referee was forthcoming Sweden would provide one. The prospect of playing in Sweden with a Swedish referee filled the Danish president with foreboding. Cleaver discovered, after agreeing, that the pitch was eight hundred miles from Copenhagen, which gave him a journey he does not care to recall, and when he got there he discovered the match was to be televised.

Although daunted at the thought of suddenly becoming an international referee in the middle of what he had thought was a relaxing summer holiday, he managed to get away with it without being lynched; the fact that each side scored a try which was converted seemed to have given pleasure all round. 'The game', he said, 'as far as I can remember, resembled a match between two English junior schools which have recently changed from Association to the handling code. I didn't have to worry much about the finer points of the game, perhaps a better knowledge of the rules (or laws) of the combined codes of Association, American and Australian would have been an asset. Anyway, everyone seemed to enjoy it, includng the crowd who hooted with laughter for the greater part of the game.'

All that was thirty years ago. The game is very popular in Scandinavia and playing standards have improved dramatically.

Dick Leonard raised the Harlequin colours in a game in Honolulu. While he was stationed in that part of the world the talk in the bar one night turned to rugger. The first game ended prematurely, for they had, inadvertently, arrived late and dusk was already imminent. By the time they finished it was almost

Harlequins v Coventry in 1964. C.M.Payne passes from the line-out.

impossible to see each other, let alone the opposing team or the ball.

Their next fixture was on the same ground but against different opponents. He wrote:

> It was an interesting ground in that it had no lines, except the touch-line, where the crowd stood, which was marked by a piece of string: the rest was left to the players' judgement. The opposing teams turned out to be composed of fourteen Tongans and a New Zealander, all playing in bare feet. These chaps played with a spirit and enjoyment that I have never before seen on a rugger field. I know now why the Fijians are so hard to beat. Their handling was miraculous and tackling them was like being run over by a train.
>
> The score? I think we'll pass over that, except to say that they can't have scored less than twelve tries. They all then went off to wrestle and play basketball. They were superbly fit and it was an object lesson in uninhibited rugger.

At the end of this unexpectedly strenuous game they were dismayed to discover that because it was a Mormon establishment no alcohol was available.

Colin Payne took over the captaincy in the Sixties. In the early stages of his Rugby Football career it seemed that he had been gifted with everything except luck. After three years in the Sherborne First XV, he did two years National Service, and therefore was slightly older than pre-war undergraduates tended to be. (Nowadays, of course, it is not unusual for 'students', as they are known, to appear at Oxford and Cambridge after attending other universities and acquiring international caps and sometimes a wife and family on the way.)

Colin was an obvious choice for a blue in his first year, but broke his collarbone (in a match against the Quins) before he could play against Cambridge. The following year he was injured again in the last game before the Varsity match.

He was almost as unlucky in English trial matches. He had played in an English trial in his early days at Oxford but injury then put him out of the reckoning. His second trial, three months later, was played in thick fog. Although large, he seems to have been invisible to the selectors. In 1964 he started to collect the first of his ten English caps.

As the Sixties malaise was lingering on, early in 1964 the captain found it necessary to strike a forceful note:

'The time has come for a few harsh words in public. What has happened to the playing strength of the club in the 'A' echelons? There is a spirit of malaise which, in my opinion, is only in the mind.

'Let us just stop and consider for the moment why things are not what they ought to be. First and foremost I get the impression from the team captains that there is a complete lack of spirit and lack of pride in the jerseys you are wearing.

'Secondly, and as important, there is a general lack of fitness. Players are not even fit enough to stay and drink after the game.

'Thirdly, and this is tied in with the team spirit, three-quarters of you couldn't really care less whether you played or not. I put it to you that just a small sacrifice for the club will repay itself in results.

'If a team is not winning, no one enjoys himself. If a team is not winning, it is not good enough just to walk out and give up. I am convinced that everyone is playing at least fifty per cent below his capabilities, merely because there is a general air of "couldn't care less". Snap out of it, gentlemen, and live up to the name of the club.

'Let's be more cheerful: the scene is not as black as all that. Much of the trouble stems from the fact that at the time of going to Press, the Quins have something like fifteen out of the top forty-five injured or unavailable through business or work. Also, the fixture list has been considerably strengthened and has taken one or two of us by surprise. Let's surprise someone else for a change.'

Rugby Football was going through a period of transition at this time. On one side of the scale was the attitude that 'it's only a game' and to show massive enthusiasm by going for long training runs was rather immature. On the other side of the scale was the increasing respect for physical fitness for its own sake. The latter attitude was fostered by the two establishments, St Luke's College, Exeter and Loughborough College.

Although the primary purpose of these two establishments was to produce instructors in physical education, the fact of having so many athletic students on the premises enabled them to produce excellent teams at a variety of games, not least Rugby Football. St Luke's won the Middlesex seven-a-sides in 1957 and Loughborough did the same in 1959. London Scottish then won for four successive years, then Loughborough were back in 1964 and 1966. Although the Quins won in 1967, St Luke's took the trophy in 1969 and Loughborough in 1970.

By that time the message that victory goes to the supremely fit seemed to have penetrated into the Rugby world. The 'couldn't care less about the result' attitude of the early Sixties seems to have blown away in the highly competitive world of today with its leagues and cup matches, and the national passion for physical fitness via jogging, marathons, aerobics and indoor sports which vary from basketball to karate.

Now perhaps we (the nation, not just the Quins) have gone too far in the pursuit of fitness and winning trophies. The next battle may be to preserve the spirit of the game, which has always been embodied in the Harlequin style of play. It is not going to be easy to maintain their style and standards in the present climate. It has been pointed out, not very kindly, that as Rugby Football is a very physical game this has meant that it has always tended to attract people with more muscle than brain power. Very appropriately, the musclemen have often decided to put something back into the game by serving on committees when their playing days are over. Although some of them are highly intelligent, there are undoubtedly many who conform to Parkinson's theory that most people are promoted to a position one step above their level of competence.

Looking back over the tinkering with the laws over the last 100 years it looks as if Parkinson's theory must be correct. This makes it absolutely vital for a club like the Harlequins (and the Quins are by no means unique) to refuse to be chivvied along by what is known as 'public opinion', that is those with the loudest voices.

At the moment Rugby Football is facing a crisis similar to that which caused the formation of Rugby League, (*ie* should star players benefit financially from their playing skills). Most people would consider that if you are lucky enough to be born with the talent to become a famous international, the privilege, pleasure and honour of being selected is a more than adequate reward in itself. Others claim that the amount of time involved in playing and training has a damaging effect on work, other forms of leisure, and, perhaps, family life. At the moment of writing the debate centres on whether a star should be paid for appearing in an advertisement. Perhaps yes, but it may be the tip of a dangerous iceberg which will eventually sink the amateurism in Rugby Football and with it the spirit of the Harlequin Football Club.

The slack period which the captain castigated in 1963 did not last long. The next year, the First XV won ten out of their first twelve matches, the Wanderers lost seven and won eight by the end of the year, and the 'A's won thirty-two and lost seven. By the time the Quins reached the Easter tour in April 1965 they had an encouraging record of playing right up to the final whistle instead of accepting a scoreline midway through the second half. At St Helen's on 17 April, Swansea established a 24-13 lead. But, as the reporter (Ron Griffiths) from the *South Wales Evening Post* put it:

> *The battling Quins were by no means finished. Wrench went away at the right-hand touch-line, and Swansea tried a clearance kick which went straight to McPartlin. He raced away and left-wing Parkin finished a fine movement with an unconventional try at the corner.*

A good effort considering that Grahame Murray was off the field for much of the match with a badly-damaged nose. It was also on the Easter tour, which is not the best preparation for stamina in the closing minute.

In 1966 the Harlequins marked their Centenary Year and therefore decided to celebrate in some style. The sequence of events planned to mark this auspicious occasion were first of all a match against Jean Prat's International XV at Twickenham on 3 September; then, a week later, a match against the Wasps on their ground at Sudbury to celebrate that club's (1867) Centenary as well. It was decided that the clubs would share the gate money between them. As we have noted earlier in this book, the Wasps were great rivals, and even greater friends, in their early days. At times, however, the two clubs have drifted apart (Quins broke off the fixtures in 1952 and did not resume them till the end of the Sixties), but the organisations are now on the best of terms and shall continue to be so (unless one upsets the other's plans for winning the Cup and the League at any time in the future).

Also in September 1966, the Quins planned to play the East African XV which was touring in England. This would be a sentimental occasion for the Quins were the first club to tour East Africa. All this, of coure, was in addition to their normal programme of matches.

On 8 October the Quins played the Athletic Club of Wellington, New Zealand, who were making a short tour of England prior to visiting Russia. The Athletic Club were the second New Zealand club to tour Britain; the first had been the Maoris, whom the Quins had defeated 11-6 in 1926, in what was described as 'a stirring encounter'.

On 9 November there was a cocktail party at the House of Commons for members, wives and friends, and on 16 November Reunion Day itself. This was held at the Stoop and was exactly what it promised to be.

On 3 December the Quins had a Centenary Dinner at the Mansion House (a great privilege), an occasion when the speeches were well above the ordinary, which was hardly surprising as Norman Birkett made one of them.

In April the Centenary Ball took place at Twickenham. For this momentous occasion the Quins had a marquee draped in Harlequin colours and music was provided by four bands. It was, as might be expected, a phenomenal success.

Centenaries, or other anniversaries, are appropriate times to take a look at the past and see it with the benefit of hindsight. All too often, though, when one takes a backward look at the history of an institution, be it a club, a school, a company, or a regiment, sentiment and emotion take precedence over proper critical assessment. We should hope to avoid this.

Players in the 1860s must have looked remarkably different from those of today. Some of the players nowadays have hair which is on the long side, but in the early days of the club short hair would have been conspicuous, not long. No doubt many of their

Harlequins v Roma in 1965. Payne (Quins) and Beitoli (Roma) jumping for the ball.

members had beards, and those who did not probably sported moustaches. Amongst their spectators there were no doubt beards which came well down on to the chest. It was the fashion in the nineteenth century to wear a lot of facial hair, often displayed in elaborately trimmed sideboards. The only factor which restrained many a player from grabbing a handful of his opponent's whiskers was the certain knowledge that the inevitable retaliation would include similar treatment of his own.

The grounds on which their early forbears performed were invariably rough fields, whose uneven surface would have been studded with tussocks of grass and occasional shallow holes. Very long grass would be mowed with a scythe. For international matches, the first of which was England v Scotland in 1891, some attempt would have been made to level the field and make it more playable, but most club games took place on fields which were chosen simply because they were less uneven than the others nearby.

Washing facilities were rudimentary, but it must be remembered that these were the days, which lasted well into the present century, when very few houses had proper bathrooms (or inside lavatories). The water supply and sewage system of London in the days when the Harlequins played their early matches were primitive.

Nevertheless, their founder members would have had an impressive appearance (after a wash in cold well water which was so hard that the soap would hardly lather). Elegant, curly-brimmed hats, high collars, colourful cravats, cutaway coats and well-tailored trousers would show that Harlequins took considerable pride in their appearance. Scent was not considered effeminate, but necessary. During the Crusades in the Middle Ages, knights who had to wear their armour for days on end used a lot of scent. It was also popular in the Western Desert in 1942, particularly among tank crews who had no water to spare for washing themselves.

Travel to matches, either home or away, must have presented considerable problems. Although there had been a mania for railway building, the routes were not always convenient for rugger matches and at least some part of the journey would need to be taken in a horse-drawn conveyance, or perhaps on the horse itself. The sight of the Harlequins emerging from a horse-drawn hansom cab must have been a cheering sight.

The telephone was not invented till 1876, and even then took some time before it became available to the general public. There was therefore no easy way of telling one's opponents not to travel because the ground was flooded or unavailable for other reasons. However, for local messages there were always plenty of errand boys only too ready to earn a few pence for walking a mile or two.

In the wider background it is worth recalling that the American Civil War was reaching its bitter end in the year the club was founded. Britain was now at the height of its imperial power — 'the empire on which the sun never sets' with the Royal Navy keeping the peace (on the seas at least) for a whole century. The difference between rich and poor was striking, as Charles Dickens made clear in his novels, but overall the spirit of the second half of the nineteenth century and into the first part of the twentieth, was that life could only become better for everyone, provided that discontented foreigners like Germans, French, Italians and Russians did not spoil it.

The British Army was usually having to deal with some trouble-maker or other in China, India, Burma, the Sudan, Africa or the West Indies, but this did not affect the average citizen until the South African War of 1899-1902. When that broke out vast numbers volunteered to fight in a conflict in which both the opposition and the terrain had been underestimated. This was the period when the Harlequins nearly ceased to exist, no doubt because most of the members had volunteered to fight overseas in a war in which more died from disease than bullets (when, it was said, the doctor killed more than the butcher).

National confidence returned in the Edwardian period and this, of course, was the start of their days of greatness, guided by Adrian Stoop and his talented colleagues. But just when it seemed that the nation and the Harlequins were poised for a very successful future, along came World War One in 1914. By the time it finished in 1918 it was clear that the world would never be the same again.

The Harlequins shook off the effects of the war in the Twenties rather more quickly than the rest of the nation did. The economy made shaky progress in the 1920s and was then hit by the great slump in 1931. As Harlequins tended to be drawn from the professions, the Services and established businesses, the Quins were less affected by the effect of the slump than many clubs elsewhere.

However, as Reg Bolton pointed out earlier, these were the days when most of their playing members found cash tight and car owners were a rarity. Some of their opponents, particularly those from the Midlands, Wales and the North, included players who had been out of work for years and lived in a state of poverty which meant that food was short and the cost of boots and shorts a major problem.

In consequence it was not unusual for a major club to provide shorts, stockings and boots and sometimes a five pound note (worth twenty times as much as it is today) in one of the boots. After a game the 'tea' consisted of something much more substantial than sandwiches and cakes. It was a way of 'looking after' your players.

Then came World War Two in 1939 and lasted for six years. Club or representative rugger was impossible: in the early days matches were banned because crowds of spectators were thought to make an attractive target for enemy bombers. There was, however, plenty of unit-level rugger available in the Services, where Rugby

Union and Rugby League players appeared alongside each other in the same team.

A start was made again in 1945. The nation as a whole was still suffering from the effects of six years of war, bombing, industrial disruption etc, and economic recovery did not begin till the Fifties. National Service (conscription) remained in force until 1962, so many of the Quins' younger members had a taste of service life in various parts of the world before being able to settle down and play for the club.

During peacetime, National Service called up men for two years; some of them saw action in wars like those in Korea or Malaya, but all those who wanted to managed to play a number of games including Rugby Football. National Service tended to give people an independent outlook and widen their interests. This meant that members who before the war would have been content to put up with certain inadequacies in the club, such as lack of opportunities for promotion to senior teams, were more inclined to try their luck elsewhere. After the 1939-45 conflict there was a more competitive attitude in sport, and clubs which did not encourage their younger members to stay were liable to find themselves hard pressed if hit by a spate of injuries. Complacency is a dangerous factor in any institution; in a Rugby Football club it is liable to be disastrous.

Although the outside world tends to regard the Harlequin Football Club as rolling in money, that view is not shared by members of the committee and, particularly, the Treasurer. A bright idea to solve the problem of the shortfall was the Harlequin 200 Club. This was simply a lottery with a membership of 200 members. By limiting the membership, each subscriber was given a better chance to secure a prize, in contrast to the sort of lottery in which millions of tickets are issued to hopefuls. Members subscribed five shillings weekly (the equivalent of about £2.50 today). There was a draw each week for a prize of ten pounds and at the end of the season there would be a draw for two prizes of £500 each. Although both subscriptions and prizes have subsequently been modified, the 200 Club continues to flourish and provides an additional source of income to the club.

Another interesting experiment which was begun in Centenary Year was 'The Third Half'. For some time past it had been noticeable that turning up to play and then disappearing after the game did nothing for club unity and friendship. In consequence players, past and present, were asked to drop in to the Stoop bar any time after five o'clock on Saturdays afternoons in the rugger season.

Great efforts were made to encourage former internationals to stay after the game they had just seen and unburden themselves of any comments they felt might be appropriate. Such criticisms are absorbed more easily when washed down with a pint or two. Although some of their brasher members were at first resentful of hearing constructive (*ie* adverse) comments on their style of play, and were inclined to regard the oldies as people who must have played the game when the ball was still a pig's bladder, the message gradually got around that some of the stone-age survivals were more in touch with the tactics of the modern game than might have been suspected from their appearance.

All in all 'The Third Half', which was run by R.F.Crichton, a pre-1939 wing-forward, was a great success, not least in the financial contribution it made to the club.

By the end of the decade the club finances were in good shape. On current account the Quins made a profit of £4,000, to which was added £2,000 from the 200 Club.

Very appropriately, the club arranged for the publications of a small booklet (or brochure) to commemorate the Centenary. It was sponsored by W.D. & H.O.Wills, the cigarette manufacturers. It had a foreword by Group-Captain G.A.Walker, who was president of the RFU in their Centenary Year. 'Gus' Walker was a diminutive fly-half who had played for England in 1939, although he had failed to win his blue when up at Cambridge (St Catharine's). He became a familiar figure as a first-class referee in the post-war years, although he had lost one arm during World War Two when a bomber crashed on the airfield he was commanding. It exploded when he was trying to rescue the aircrew.

Although a Blackheath man, Walker had a great respect and affection for the Harlequins, with whom he felt that Wakefield had probably done as much for attacking forward play as Stoop had for reorganising the backs. He wrote: 'As one who has been privileged to play against and referee the Quins on many occasions, I can testify to the fact that succeeding Quins have striven and succeeded in playing enterprising, open, attacking Rugby'. He commented, in particular, on the excellent influence the Harlequins have had 'wherever Rugby is played throughout the world'.

Geoffrey Nicholson, the well-known newspaper correspondent, wrote an article entitled 'Hartlequins in the Corps d'Élite'. He quoted a book entitled *The Rugby Union Game*, which had been compiled by the Revd Francis Marshal and was published in 1892, it said of the Quins of that date:

Any Saturday they can put three teams out in the field, and

*with such materials at hand they require only some Yorkshire
stingo to place them far higher in the scale of success. It is
one of the few London clubs which is endowed with a large
amount of esprit de corps.*

Francis had gone on to say that the Quins were not the most
fashionable of London clubs at the time, for Blackheath, Richmond
and the London Scottish all had more glamour and influence;
international matches were played at Blackheath and Richmond.
It was not surprising that the Quins never hosted an international
match, they were hard put to find a suitable setting for their own
games, as we have seen.

Nicholson commented sadly that although Leake was their first
official international, three other Harlequins had been capped for
England earlier; unfortunately one (Wilkinson) was listed as
playing for the Law Society and the other two had moved to
Blackheath before they were capped. The Yorkshire stingo to which
Francis had referred was that dark beer which now only seems
to be available in small bottles, usually under the title of 'barley
wine' or a similar euphemism. It was still very popular as a draught
beer in the Thirties and was brewed in many Oxford and Cambridge
colleges. One and a half pints was usually enough to put the average
drinker under the table; one wonders what a whiff of it would
do to a breathalyser bag.

Nicholson informs us that Adrian Stoop apparently listed sixteen
different ways in which forwards and backs could combine to attack.
(How many of them are used nowadays, one might profitably ask?)

However, *The Times* of 1892 took a sourer view of Harlequin
creativity: 'The only really new principle they have set up is the
value of unorthodoxy *per se*, the intrinsic worth of the unexpected
move as an attacking factor, simply because it is unexpected'.

This comment, one should remember, was made some fifteen
years before Adrian put his ideas into practice.

Ricky Bartlett also contributed an article and made a point which
many would echo twenty-five years later:

*I do not think the lawmakers have helped the open game.
In the old days when the ball had to be played with the foot
after a tackle the Quins had many more loose scrums. Forwards
broke from the tight, saw a tackle taking place, and accelerated
to strive for possession in the ensuing maul. Now, when the
forward sees the tackle, he runs deep to cover the attack arising
from the quick pick up. Thus, even when the initial thrust
is stopped, the "second-phase attack" is running into cover
in depth.*

At its best, their play of the Fifties produced long flowing moves with forwards running and passing confidently with the backs, but on their blacker days their attempt to demonstrate 'Harlequin Football' seemed like a scrambled version of basketball, moving sometimes sideways but mostly backwards. Such a style of play depends on all fifteen players having confidence in the group ability to open the game from almost any point in the game. This can only be gained by sticking to the policy of open play and slowly gaining confidence.

He pointed out that in the past the Quins usually had backs who were superior to their opponents. This was no longer always true: furthermore opposing teams often came into the field with well thought-out tactical plans against which a little casual Harlequin improvisation might not be too successful.

Finally, he emphasised the need for proficiency in basic skills such as passing, catching, tackling and kicking. 'However skilful the tactics are, the success ultimately depends on the execution of the basic skills.'

Cliff Morgan, the famous Welsh stand-off half, who played twenty-nine times for Wales, and has since become a greatly respected broadcaster on many subjects as well as Rugby Football, gave a perceptive tribute:

'They do even go as far as to say that William Webb Ellis was a Quin, do them Arlequins . . . The Welshman who uttered these words was, like many other people I know, jealous of the proudest of clubs, one steeped in the tradition of 100 glorious years.

'Let me straightway confess that before I played against, and was soundly beaten by, the Harlequin team of 1950, that I too nurtured a little resentment. The club appeared, from a distance, to represent everything my Celtic (or rather Iberian) forefathers fought against: Conservative, old school tie, and above all else, English, with English players with cultured English accents. Time, thank goodness, has destroyed my immature image. Now my approach is realistic.

'Few club matches in which I played for Cardiff provided as much fun as the Harlequin fixture. Absent was the inevitable tension of the close club rivalry of Welsh football, indeed there was a genuine demand by the Harlequins to attack the opposition with all the facilities available.

'Indeed, one thing the Cardiff backs always envied was the way the Harlequin forwards were capable of the fast, clean heel from the "Loose".

'What I found when playing the Quins was that their approach was right, it was positive which meant you could play positive Rugby against them.

'The Harlequins, of course, pioneered floodlit Rugby, as indeed they did tours into Europe some years ago. I know that Rugby "under the lights" and behind the "Curtain" is not to everyone's liking at Rugby headquarters. This is really important. What really matters is that both were a challenge to the Harlequins, a challenge accepted with dignity.

'It was this dignity both on and off the field that made the boys I knew first-class company. Perhaps more than any other though, Ricky Bartlett. It's not until another fly-half makes you look second best that you really respect him. Ricky did this to me on two memorable occasions. I respected, and still respect him for, apart from his playing, his approach epitomises what a rugger man should be.

'In a dressing-room at Cardiff Arms Park in 1950, Adrian Stoop had a long chat with me. Apart from telling me how to play fly-half he convinced me that a painful back injury I had at the time was all in my mind. He told me the most difficult opponent you meet is yourself. How right he was. What a lesson. What a man!'

John Reason, of the *Daily Telegraph*, indicated the difficulties that the Harlequins were already facing and which were likely to increase in the future:

'Just as brighter cricket means a studied attempt to hit fours and sixes all over the place, so open Rugby means a studied attempt to score tries all over the place. In the final analysis it means that the spectator wants to see a game in which attack is given more emphasis, than defence, though only so long as his side wins. Attack is honourable, defence is something less, so right must prevail.

'Even the briefest study of Rugby Football, or any other game for that matter, will show that among those who watch the sport this has been a long felt want, and the Harlequins, bless their hearts, have done their best to supply it. Great players have come to the club down the years and they have *attacked*.'

However, John Reason went on to point out that 'since 1945 the most significant advances in the tactical thinking about the game have been in defence . . .Rugby football is not alone in facing this problem.'

In all games, he noted, but particularly in cricket 'defence is now eighty-five per cent of the game . . .It has not come to that in Rugby Football yet but you have only to read the Rugby Union's excellent new coaching manual to realise that defensive techniques are now so sophisticated that indiscriminate attack is quite simply

R.F.Read, the Harlequins fly-half, avoids a tackle by W.McDowell of the Athletic Club (New Zealand) at Twickenham in 1966.

bad Rugby. The open game regrettaby is wide open. It is too vulnerable . . .

'The Harlequins were able to play their traditional game in the past because they had players who were not only good enough, but in most cases who were that vital bit better than their opponents. They had to be to get away with it, because playing an open game even then involved risks which could only be overcome by players who had a margin of superiority.

'That margin has gone . . .

'The Harlequins do not have the best players in Britain to choose from, so how much more difficult it must be for their players to sustain their traditional style of play against teams who have not the slightest intention of playing open football and who are fortified by the knowledge that the old idea of open football is no longer accepted as good play in any case.'

He added: 'The Harlequins face another difficulty as well. I think it is fair to say that the richest recruiting grounds for the club have always been the Universities of Oxford and Cambridge and until about three years ago those universities produced some of the best players in the country. Unfortunately, this no longer applies and if the present miserable obsession with academic ability continues, the alarming decline in the standard of Rugby Football at those two universities will also continue . . .Therefore, the Harlequins will have to look elsewhere for their players. That sentence is easy enough to write, but it amounts to no less than a revolution, and a sombre one at that.'

Fortunately this shrewd prediction has not been entirely fulfilled. University football is still producing some good players although not in the numbers they did before. And, after some decidedly unhappy periods, their successes in Cup, League and seven-a-sides have helped greatly in recruiting.

In the Centenary Year, W.W.Wakefield, now Lord Wakefield of Kendal, was president, R.T.Kindred was chairman, and G.C.Murray captain of the club. W.Wiggins was secretary, assisted by P.C.Forbes, and G.S.Hamilton was treasurer. The trustees were A.A.Moller, H.J.Gould and K.H.Chapman. The committee consisted of G. de Bruyne, P.M.Meaney, V.G.Roberts, R.F.Crichton, P.C.Orr, D.A.Whiting, R.W.D.Marques, C.M.Payne, D.R.Williams and R.S.Relf.

The Wanderers team was captained by J.Hancock, and the 'A's by W.S.Gibbs, R.C.Carr and A.P.Dagleas. The team secretary for the First XV and the Wanderers was J.Seldon and for the 'A' XVs was M.J.Hollins. H.J.Gould was fixtures secretary for the First XV and H.G.Thomas was fixtures secretary for the Wanderers and the 'A's. All these appointments were, of course, honorary and often involved the holder in a lot of unrecoverable (even if wanted) personal expenses.

Unfortunately *Harlequinade* went into abeyance in 1970, when its staff took a well-earned rest and looked around for volunteers to take their places. Apart from the time taken to produce the magazine, there was the major problem of increasing expenses. However, its absence was so widely deplored that in 1987 it was reborn.

Into the Depths and Out Again

EVERY club has its 'downs', and after the euphoria which attended their centenary celebrations it was inevitable that the Quins should run into stormy weather. There was no real reason why the Harlequins should have taken the downturn that they took in the Seventies but it happened just the same.

The Quins began the decade with a sprinkling of internationals. At full-back there was R.'Bob' Hiller, who was first capped for England in 1968 and went on to play nineteen more times. Bob Hiller was worth his place in the national side for his playing abilities alone but it was as a kicker that he was best known. Hiller's long pause after he had placed the ball used to raise the tension in the crowd to almost hysterical levels. Originally he had taken a lengthy time to collect his thoughts and concentrate, but later he would sometimes do it in order to needle the crowd if they were then booing and cat-calling.

Hiller had been spotted by David Brooks when playing in a Surrey junior game. He was surprised to be invited to join the Harlequins for up until then the height of his ambition had been to play for Bec Old Boys. Subsequently he toured South Africa with the British Lions and when out there set a new points scoring record both for the tour and in an individual match. He became captain of England in 1969. He had a BSc degree from Birmingham University and he went to Oxford in 1965 on a post-graduate course, where he won a rugger and cricket blue.

N.C.'Nigel' Starmer-Smith was playing alongside Hiller when he won the first of his seven caps against South Africa in 1969. Starmer-Smith was very much an Oxford man for he was educated at Magdalen College School there before entering the University. He was reserve for England seven times before being capped. He began his working life as a schoolmaster at Epsom College, but later moved to the BBC where he became a regular commentator on international matches.

Also in the backs the Quins had R.H.'Bob' Lloyd at left centre; he was capped four times for England. The pack was a formidable proposition with a front row of Grahame Murray (a trialist but never capped), P.C.'Pat' Orr, and David Wrench who had been capped back in 1964.

Behind these were N.O.'Nick' Martin, who had played for Cambridge for three years, packing down alongside A.M.'Mike' Davis, who would eventually play for England seventeen times. Martin would also be capped later. At number-eight was the formidable presence of Colin Payne. Unfortunately, some of these were reaching the end of their Rugby careers. Mike Davis, however, would return to the club later as coach, a post he managed to combine, miraculously, with being a housemaster at Sherborne, 120 miles away. Bob Hiller was still playing for England in the 1971-72 season and captained the team against France. The *Playfair Rugby Football Annual* became quite lyrical about his performances:

It's That Man Again . . .the name of Hiller will become a permanent nightmare to the Rugby footballers of Ireland. Hiller kicked three penalty goals by which Ireland were beaten, despite scoring two themselves. (A try then counted for three points). Hiller's record against the unfortunate Irish is worthy of close scrutiny. In four matches against Ireland he has kicked nine penalty goals, two in 1968 at Twickenham, four at Lansdowne Road in 1969 and three in this match. Add to this his incredible dropped goals against them at Twickenham in 1970. Hiller seems to have become the player who has done Ireland more damage than any single player they have ever met.

The report on the England-France game which was a 14-14 draw was headlined 'Hiller plays France'. It went on:

What can be said about Hiller that is new, only that he confirms time and time again that if he has any fallibilities they must be accepted on their face value, but he must be included in any English side for his kicking. France were robbed of their due deserts purely and simply by Hiller. It is almost as if it were worthwhile for him to read a book on the touchline for the afternoon and just come on the field for the kicks, except this time he threw in a try for good measure.

Hiller reminded the French of his presence and just what his capabilities were after barely a couple of minutes play; after meticulously building his large mound of earth and doing his breathing exercises for some seconds before beginning his short

run-up and stabbing kick, Hiller sent the ball sailing between the posts from some thirty yards.

By the end of this game Bob Hiller had scored 101 points out of the 157 England had scored in fourteen internationals.

However, even with Hiller, C.B.'Stack' Stevens, P.J.Dixon and N.Starmer-Smith, the Quins had a poorish season in which losses and wins were roughly equal. Stack Stevens had come to us from Penzance-Newlyn and was first capped for England in 1969. By 1975 he had been capped twenty-four more times. Peter Dixon had played for Oxford against Cambridge for four successive years. He went on to win twenty-two caps. He also played for Gosforth.

The Seventies had seen the introduction of the knock-out cup, at that time sponsored by John Player Limited, soon to be followed by the Courage National League system. These two innovations made a difference to Rugby Football that amounted to a revolution. Suddenly the whole national game became more competitive and it soon became clear that if a club was not in the First Division of the League it became much less attractive to spectators. The question which worried a lot of people was whether the Harlequins would be able to continue to play in their attractive carefree style in this new world of highly competitive rugger.

The Harlequins did not reach the Final of the John Player Cup (which began in 1972) until 1988, when they won it by defeating Bristol 28-22. However, the club has always managed to stay in the First Division of the Courage League and avoid the fate of some of their contemporaries, like Blackheath, Richmond and London Scottish, who have had to struggle in Division Two.

When Harlequins are contemplating how far they may indulge in attractive rugger, as opposed to winning grimly, they bring up the name of London Welsh. A few years ago the London Welsh were a by-word for attractive and successful Rugby. Quite suddenly their older players retired and new talent seemed to be scarce. From being the most dynamic club in London, the unfortunate Welsh sank quite rapidly until they dropped into Division Four (South).

Although it still retained most of its original fixture for 'friendly' (*ie* non-League) games, it was clear that recovery, if ever, would be slow and arduous. The London Scottish once fell to Division Three, but by a heroic effort hoisted themselves up to Division Two again. Faced by such unpleasant facts, the Quins decided that playing open, attractive Rugby Football in League games was a luxury they could ill afford. The hard facts of life were that

*Opposite: Bob Hiller in action on the British
Lions tour to New Zealand in 1971.*

if you were not in the First Division you were unlikely to attract the calibre of recruits to get you up there.

At best the First Division was a very slippery slope and any club in the bottom half in mid-season would spend a lot of time anxiously looking over its shoulder. Even so, as far as possible, and sometimes even further than has been wise, the Quins have tried to play in traditional style.

For reasons which no one seems able to identify, for there was nothing wrong with the captaincy or the amount of talent available, the club seemed to be going into slow decline during the Seventies. However, before decline became disaster, the Quins were saved by a new arrival on the scene. This was Dick Best who, after captaining the club, introduced new training and team-building methods.

In the 1978-79 report it had been said: 'There have been considerable inconsistencies in the team's performances which must stem from a lack of individual and collective discipline (using the word in its widest sense). The essentials for next season are the development of personal and team routines and disciplines, and the attraction of established players to strengthen the first-team squad.'

However, the season had seen 'a notable debut by John Butcher'.

The Wanderers, who had so often enjoyed high praise for their performance, had fallen behind during the season. This was partly due to injuries but was also attributed to a lack of commitment. There was an incredible statistic, 'over sixty players had turned out for the Wanderers but only six players had taken part in more than half of the fixtures'. With this situation in the Wanderers it was hardly surprising that the First XV was hard-pressed when looking for reserves. That season the Firsts won eleven matches and lost nineteen, the Wanderers won nine and lost fifteen, the 'A's won forty and lost fourteen, and the Colts won thirteen and lost three.

The 1979-80 season began with ominous portent. At the annual meeting the Committee's nominated Captain was outvoted and A.C.Alexander elected in his place. No doubt Alexander would have been a great success in that capacity but unfortunately he departed to Rugby League in December; in 1991 he was reinstated to the Rugby Football Union.

Over the years the Harlequins have not lost many players to Rugby League, but it has not been through lack of approaches, mainly over the telephone, by Rugby League scouts. Perhaps the most spectacular approach was that allegedly made to England

The Harlequins front row goes into battle, cheerfully but warily.

captain Will Carling in May 1991, when it was reported in the national Press that he had turned down a £1 million offer to sign for Leeds RLFC.

T.C.Claxton took over the captaincy in December 1979 and led the club to the semi-final of the John Player Cup, where they lost to Leicester, the eventual winners of the competition. Fortunately for the Quins they had the assistance of A.M.Haden, the New Zealander who eventually played in forty-one Test Matches for the All Blacks, as well as in over a hundred games which were not Tests. They also had a very lively back row, consisting of D.H.Cooke, P.D.Jackson and E.Weekes.

The Wanderers established a new but unenviable record of having *seventy-five* players turn out for them during the season. In consequence they won twelve and lost eighteen of their matches. They were captained by J.N.Whipp, who coped admirably with what can only be described as a mobile situation.

The 'A's, some of whose players had begun the season with a tour in Holland, had a remarkable successful season, although many of their players were called up by the Wanderers, and even, on occasions, by the First XV. The Quins' convention that no one would be elected who was not capable of playing in the First, if needs be, was fully justified this season. The Colts, who were managed by Tom Inwood, assisted by A.R.Mason and H.J.Gould, won eleven and lost only four matches.

One of the strange conventions of Rugby Football reports is that the medics are never mentioned. This seems to be taking professional anonymity too far, for many a game has been saved by an instant diagnosis on whether the player is fit to continue or will drop dead if he does. Equipped with nothing but their own commonsense and judgement, and under the critical gaze of twenty-nine players and several thousand spectators, the responsibility of the medics is awesome. Nevertheless R.A.Rossdale, L.Walkden and M.J.Hollins served the Quins well in their respective honorary capacities.

The club was were lucky to have the assistance and advice of E.W.Kirton, with the invaluable experience he had gained by playing fifteen times for the All Blacks, that year; one shudders to think what the club's record would have been like without him.

Financially, the Quins were holding their own; the 200 Club, the bars and not least the gate money making a useful addition to the income from subscriptions.

An interesting development at this time was the restoration of many of the club's old photographs by I.Johnson. As most people know, there comes a time in the life of a photograph when, if it is not preserved, it disappears for ever. Fortunately, the Harlequins' ancient archives have now avoided that fate.

Lord Wakefield was still the club's president, and J.D.Currie was chairman. R.F.Looker had now taken over the duties of secretary from J.Seldon, who had by now given many years of invaluable assistance to the club. Another retirement was that of Jay Gould, who had served the club for fifty years.

During 1980-81, the club was still trying to heave itself out of the trench it had dug for itself, but the process looked like taking longer than had been expected. The First XV won sixteen and lost eighteen matches: five were drawn. The Wanderers broke even, winning thirteen, losing thirteen and drawing one. The 'A's won forty-five, lost twenty-two and drew two. The Colts record looked rather dismal on the surface, but when it is realised that there were barely enough players for one XV at the beginning of the season, yet the club finished with two, one under-19 and the other under-17, the picture looked more encouraging.

From the Firsts, D.H.Cooke was capped for England, and C.Butcher played for England under-23. K.M.Bushell was chosen as full-back for England 'B'.

One of the most constructive aspects of this season was the guiding presence among the 'A's of such seasoned campaigners as M.J.Whiteside, R.Hiller, G.C.Murray, K.G.Jones, J.P.Gronow and D.R.Williams.

Many of the Quins' fellow clubs have built success on grooming players in what might be called the junior sides (although some are actually older than their seniors). It looked as if the Harlequins were about to follow the same path and not to rely so much on attracting already mature players. It is, of course, much easier, if you are a provincial club, to train and retain players from your local catchment area. In London, with its mobile population and several first-class clubs within a mile or two of each other, it is not so simple.

After thirty years as president of the Harlequin FC, Lord Wakefield felt it was time to retire. His resignation was reluctantly accepted and he became patron. Ken Chapman agreed to accept the Committee's nomination of him as the new president. Ken had already become the father-figure of the Harlequins, having been captain, honorary secretary and chairman. Earle Kirton agreed to accept the vice-presidency of the club. He had now been with the Quins for ten years, including one as captain and many more as coach. Three of the club's other New Zealanders were capped for the All Blacks this season: they were A.M.Haden, N.Allen and B.Frazer.

A development which had often been discussed but which looked as if it would never come to anything was the opportunity to play squash at the Stoop. Squash is an excellent game for sharpening people up and getting them on their toes and the club was therefore delighted when they heard that a firm called 'On-line Leisure' was about to open courts at the Stoop and give special facilities to Quins players. They were even more pleased to hear that the club would be managed by T.D.Gathercole, a former First XV wing three-quarter and a very distinguished squash player.

The 1981-82 rugger season saw the Harlequins beginning to edge forward again. The Firsts, who had had the benefit, or at least privilege, of an early training weekend in France, eventually won more matches than it lost, (nineteen won, sixteen lost and one drawn). The high spots were beating Llanelli, Swansea (the first English club to win there for four years), Leicester, Wasps, London Welsh, Blackheath and Rosslyn Park.

The Quins reached the quarter-finals of the John Player Cup but then lost to Coventry after they had begun by establishing a twelve-point lead. Experience should have told them that Coventry tend to get better as the game progresses and usually manage to turn on a sort of mini-whirlwind in the last ten minutes.

However, subsequent performances showed that the lesson had not been lost on the Quins. Dick Best was the captain this year and the results of his particular talent, team building and leading, began to show. To help him he had Bill Cuthbertson, showing the consistent form which would win him twenty-two caps for Scotland. The Quins also had G.Birkett, who had been capped for Scotland in 1975, David Cooke, who was currently playing for England, and Hugh McHardy, who many thought should have been playing for Scotland. Ray Dudman was the full-back; his well-placed long kicks delighted the crowd and made his fellow players grateful.

The Wanderers may be said to have had a better season in that they only used seventy players instead of the record number of the previous season. They managed to win nine, draw two and lose fifteen of their matches. The club ran three 'A' teams and all performed creditably: A1 won fifteen, lost seven and drew one; A2 won seven, lost seven and drew one; A3 won fifteen, drew none, and lost only three. The Colts under-19s won fourteen, drew one and lost five matches; and the Colts under-17s struck an even balance by winning four and losing four, although in doing so they scored 130 points against 89.

Social activity during the season was considerable. The annual dinner was held for the first time in the entirely appropriate setting of the Whitbread Brewery in Chiswell Street. It was a great success. The annual reunion, which was organised single-handed by John Scott, went well, though the numbers were a little down that year. A New Year's Eve dance and a 'bull's blood' evening also pleased everyone.

The new squash club was officially named the Twickenham Squash Club. Not only was it a benefit for members, but the rent paid to the Quins for the premises were a useful addition to Harlequin finance. Completion of this project was largely due to Sir Patrick Meaney, mentioned earlier as the first of the Quins' non-playing elections.

There was, inevitably, a lot of committee work behind the scenes. In one's playing days one is vaguely aware that someone has to arrange that there will be opponents on the appointed day, that there will be a referee, and a ball, some hot water for a bath after the match, and some tea. One comes to take all these for granted. The more thoughtful players may wonder who collects the gate money, arranges for the jerseys to be supplied and subsequently washed, makes sure the bars are properly and securely stocked and that the car-park is not under water.

But these activities are only the tip of the iceberg. There is a vast amount of administration in every club and it is particularly heavy when a club has taken over a new ground, such as the Harlequins at the Stoop. Ground and club house maintenance is a continuing headache because costs always seem to be rising and fresh, unexpected, demands for expenditure are constantly cropping up. John Moore-Gillon was the chairman of the committee dedicated to this aspect of the club's affairs; owing to their sterling efforts, the facilities at the Stoop continued to improve, rather than lurch unsteadily from inadequate to disastrous.

Even so, with all the voluntary work, fund-raising activities and increasing membership, there was still a shortfall of income and expenditure. Reluctantly, the club agreed to raise the subscription by twenty-five per cent: even then, it was only £15 for full, and £5 for Rule XX, members.

In the 1982-83 season, the revival continued. They began well and became better and better. The First XV won twenty-two, lost thirteen and drew three games; the Wanderers won eighteen and lost ten; the 'A's won thirty-one, lost twenty-six and drew three; and the Colts (one side only) won ten and lost ten.

By now the Quins had adopted the modern system of having a First XV 'squad' system. By this it was hoped that they could occasionally rest or rotate players, be less disorganised when key players were injured, and by accustoming the reserves to the faster pace of First XV play, achieve more cohesion.

A player suddenly promoted from the Wanderers or the 'A' was hardly likely to do himself justice in his initial First XV match. This could well apply to a wing three-quarter who might never get a reasonable pass enabling him to show his speed. In the days when wings used to throw in from touch, it was sometimes said at the end of a game that the only time they touched the ball was when they threw it in to the line-out. This was less likely to happen in the Quins than in other games, notably hard-fought internationals, but it could happen to us also.

In this, as in other years, the club was often seen at its best in the smaller, but none the less difficult, seven-a-side competitions. These rarely receive any publicity and are completely overshadowed by the Middlesex Sevens and the Quins' own invitation competition, but they give a lot of pleasure to many people and, when they win, enhance the Harlequin reputation. In this season the club won the Sevenoaks, Surrey, East Grinstead and Old Belvedere competitons, but failed to get further than the semi-finals in the Middlesex Sevens.

The largest set-back that season was the departure of Roger Looker to the United States. Roger is a merchant banker but in the Quins' eyes, his main importance was that he was, first of all, a powerful prop forward, and secondly, a most efficient secretary.

Fortunately, the club now had Colin Herridge, who was already chairman of the playing committee. He agreed to combine both these time-consuming tasks. Colin, who was a scrum-half, had come to the club via Nottingham and Rosslyn Park. When he had been secretary for a few months, it was decided that if he would carry on long enough to become the longest-serving honorary secretary in the history of the club, then that would suit the Quins very well. Whether it would suit him as well might be another matter.

The only shadow on the horizon was that the Quins were still running a deficit financially. It was clear that the best way to clear this was by attracting more spectators. The task would not be easy, for there was a lot of competition for spectators in south-west London. The more games won, particularly in the Cup competitions, the bigger the 'gate' would become. However, the price of success must not be the abandonment of Harlequin-style Rugby. The Quins looked forward to the next season with keen anticipation.

Their hopes were justified. In 1983-84, the First XV won twenty-five matches and lost thirteen; the Wanderers won eighteen and lost thirteen; the 'A's won forty-four, lost twenty-one and drew three; the Under-21 XV won four, lost four and drew one; and the Colts won twelve, lost five and drew two.

At this period, the club was involved in the National and London Merit Tables, which have now been superseded by the League. The fact that some games were Merit Table games put a certain amount of needle into them but did not catch the imagination of spectators or players in the way the League has done: there is therefore no point in dwelling on the Merit Tables.

David Cooke was the club captain and led the Quins well, although it was only one of several commitments, which included the England squad, London, and Middlesex. Bill Cuthbertson, the vice-captain, was a 'regular' for Scotland, except when prevented from playing by injury. The club coach this year was Iestyn Thomas, who made an invaluable impact on Quins' performances.

The Harlequins were pleased to be told by their opponents that in spite of modern-day pressures, they were still keeping up the Harlequin traditional style of play. For this, they had reason to be grateful to some newcomers, such as Willie Jefferson, the American Eagle whose pace was described as 'blistering'. Chris Butcher played his usual sparkling game and was chosen for the England tour of South Africa. Amongst others who often caught the eye were Richard Cramb, who would later play for Scotland, Adrian Thompson, Jamie Salmon, and Everton Weekes. Alex Woodhouse and Graham Halsey also looked full of promise for the future.

County football, which was now being played on Saturdays (in spite of protests) often disrupted both the First XV and the Wanderers. Previously, county games in the south of England had taken place on Wednesdays; in the north it had been the custom to play them on Saturdays and, as northern counties had often won the County Championship, this seemed to be a sign that they took county football more seriously.

During the next few years there would be a huge restructuring of the county programme. There was a certain amount of sulking at first. Coventry and other clubs suggested to their players that club games should have priority in players' minds and even went so far as to refuse to let county games take place on their grounds.

Eventually there was another upheaval when Divisional Championships were introduced and these down-graded the county games even further. However, at the time of writing, Divisional Championships are seen by some people as a waste of time and they hope that the counties are coming back into favour.

The Quins, of course, are the main suppliers of players to Middlesex and Surrey, which counties are now challenging the formerly all-conquering Gloucestershire and Lancashire teams. However, on the Saturdays on which county matches are played, so many Quins are called up by their counties that the club can lose at least two complete teams. In general, the chief sufferers from county matches are the Wanderers. In theory, playing well for your county could be a step to higher honours; this has not often been true in the past but may become so in the future. One side effect of having a lot of Harlequins playing for different counties is that they may attract promising recruits to the club.

There were two particularly sad events this season: Lord Wakefield and Ricky Bartlett died. W.W or 'Wakers', as he was widely known, had made a great impact on the club in his playing days and in later life did his utmost to improve the game as a whole and the club in particular. He used to recall that in his playing days scrums had been formed on the 'first up, first down' principle, but he himself had introduced the idea of specialisation in the forwards.

He had played thirty-one times for England when a good total of caps was hard to come by. He was a large, strong, man and phenomenally fast for his size. Since metrication, achievements on the track are difficult to compare but he could run a quarter of a mile in 'evens', *ie* fifty seconds, which was a top-rate performance. If he had given more time to Athletics he would undoubtedly have been of Olympic standard.

He was also a top-class swimmer and sub-aqua diver, an excellent cricketer and a squash player of repute. He was a brilliant skier, both on snow and water. It seemed entirely appropriate when he became president of the Ski Club of Great Britain, but even his greatest admirers would hardly have expected him to return to competition skiing after two replacement hip operations: he did though. He was also president of the British Sub Aqua Club and president of the British Water Ski Federation.

During World War One, Wakefield had served in the Royal Naval Air Service (Fleet Air Arm) and was mentioned in dispatches. He

Opposite: J.L.B 'Jamie' Salmon, who played
for the All Blacks and then England.

153

was the first pilot to land an aeroplane on a ship (HMS Vindictive). He transferred to the RAF, from which he retired in 1923. In 1939 he rejoined the RAF, hoping to fly operationally, but instead was appointed director of the Air Training Corps, a government organisation for the selection of promising schoolboys for aircrew training.

In 1935 he had won Swindon for the Conservatives and continued to represent that constituency until he transferred to St Marylebone, which he represented from 1945 until 1963. He held three appointments as Parliamentary Private Secretary to Ministers, and but for World War Two and the Labour victory in 1945, would no doubt have become a Minister himself. He was also an extremely successful businessman.

Ricky Bartlett's death from cancer at the age of fifty-five was a profound shock to the club and to his many friends. We have referred to his style and achievements many times in these pages and it only remains to add that he was also an England selector, president of the Surrey RFU and, of course, a member of the Quins' committee.

The year 1984 brought changes to the club's fixture list. Orrell, who had been making a great name for themselves in Lancashire, came in; but the traditional Easter Monday fixture against Cardiff came out, Bridgend taking their place. The Harlequins would continue to play Cardiff home and away but a number of the Quins' other double fixtures would have to be looked at carefully in view of the club's new commitments.

The statistics for the 1984-85 season are:

	Won	Lost	Drew	For	Agn
First XV	16	16	1	625	504
Wanderers	18	9	0	580	432
'A' XVs	16	20	3	569	553
Under-21 XV	11	7	0	365	163
Under 19 XV	2	2	1	59	45

An interesting aspect of these figures is that the Quins seem to have been better at scoring points than winning matches, anomalous though that may appear. Thus the First, although winning and losing an equal number of matches, scored 120 more points than their opponents. The 'A's, although losing four more matches than they won, scored sixteen points more than their opponents; the Under-19s also outscored their opponents, although breaking even in results, whilst the Under-21s, although winning only four more matches than they lost, notched up a surplus of 202 points.

C.R.Jacobs presents the Wavell Wakefield trophy to Graham Birkett in 1983, after the Quins' first win in their own sevens.

The verdict on the Firsts was like that on thousands of schoolboy reports: 'Could do better'. A good start against the French Barbarians seemed to portend an all-conquering future. As it was, the season became one of mediocrity enlivened by highlights. David Cooke distinguished himself playing for England and also for Middlesex, who won the County Championship. Jamie Salmon frequently deputised for Cooke and Chris Butcher played for England against Australia; Bill Cuthbertson and Iain Milne distinguished themselves for Scotland.

Adrian Thompson, Marcus Rose, and Paul Curtis were in the England squad, Stuart Thresher and Mark Fletcher appeared for the England Under-23s, and Richard Cramb played for Scotland Under-21s against Holland 'B'. Willie Jefferson played for the USA.

The Wanderers, who won twelve out of their first thirteen games, were clearly back to their earlier form. The 'A's were given a slightly different nomenclature and the A1 would have had a better record if it had not been raided so heavily to make up gaps in the Wanderers. The A2 consisted of older members who were unwilling to give up playing in spite of the messages their legs kept on sending

Above: the Quins' First XV squad pictured in 1984-5. Opposite page: Graham Halsey, supported by Jamie Salmon, in a John Player Cup game in 1985.

them, but also included a number of highly promising youngsters who could quicken up the proceedings.

At the end of the season the club's accounts showed that the Quins had slipped into the red by £277. This was hardly surprising in view of the cost of improvements and maintenance. Steadily but surely, the Quins were developing the amenities of the Stoop, which included reseeding pitches and refurbishing the clubhouse. A continuing irritation and a drain on resources was vandalism to fences and other club property. This, unfortunately, is a fact of modern life and there seems to be no way to prevent it.

The 1985-86 season saw the playing record improve, but not as much as the Quins would have wished. The bare facts were:

	Won	Lost	Drew	For	Agn
First XV	18	13	0	562	416
Wanderers	18	8	0	557	347
A1	15	5	0	444	190
A2	11	7	3	388	265
Jaguars (Under-21)	21	0	0	429	139
Under-19	5	1	1	140	40

Although the First had begun the season with a tour of Northern Spain and Southern France, this did not give the Quins the winning start for which they had hoped. The general feeling about the season's results was that, as the Quins had five internationals to call on, they should have been considerably better. They reached ·the quarter-finals of the John Player Cup and then were put out by their old friends and rivals, Leicester. One of our acquisitions this season was M.P.'Micky' Skinner, a flanker; he would subsequently play a number of storming games for England.

The Wanderers maintained their improved form but everything was overshadowed by the Jaguars, who romped through the season without a defeat. There was undobutedly some exceptional talent in the Jaguars, and it was fervently hoped that when the members passed the under-21 mark they would stay with the club and not seek their fortunes elsewhere. They finished their season with an Easter tour in Holland.

At the end of the year the Quins were in the black again financially, this time with a surplus of £1,687, and it was achieved with no reduction in expenditure.

In 1986-87 the results were as follows:

	Won	Lost	Drew	For	Agn
First XV	27	12	1	768	474
Wanderers	22	7	1	774	346
A1	27	1	0	946	230

A2: Detailed results not available, but overall successful.

Jaguars	26	2	2	734	216

Under-19s: Detailed results not available, but also successful.

In view of the amount of talent available, the First XV results were disappointing, particularly as the season had begun impressively and the Quins won many hard games. As the Wanderers used seventy-two players, their results were remarkably good. Charles Van de Merwe captained the Wanderers for the second successive season before returning to South Africa. The Jaguars were again the most successful of all the teams run by the club and did well to maintain their excellent record in spite of stiffer opposition. A very healthy development was the fact that the Jaguars from now on would be regarded not as a team in isolation but a stepping stone to the First XV.

When recording the events of an earlier year, we mentioned that Micky Skinner showed the potential of an England player; this year he progressed to England 'B': older members blenched at the

Opposite: Micky Skinner, as cheerful as ever, progressed to the England 'B' team.

length of his hair but had nothing but admiration for his playing skills. Their grandfathers, of course, might have thought that Micky's hair was a bit on the short side.

Marcus Rose and Jamie Salmon appeared in the England side, both having taken a circuitous route to get there. Marcus, who had begun his education at Loughborough Grammar School, from there proceeded to Durham University and then to Cambridge; at the latter he played a season for England but was then dropped. He played for Leicester, then Coventry and then Rosslyn Park. He joined the Harlequins in 1984. This was obviously a wise move, for he soon became England's full-back once more. He is a chartered surveyor.

Jamie Salmon had travlled even further. After education at Wellington, he went out to New Zealand where they recognised his talent and selected him for the All Blacks (four times) in 1981. In 1985, having returned to England (and the Quins), he began to build up a tally of caps for England, beginning with two against the All Blacks (!) in 1986 and adding another ten, beginning with Wales in 1986 and ending with Wales in 1987.

The Quins were also fortunate to have the services of Dave Loveridge, the New Zealand scrum-half, this season. He had made over twenty appearances for the All Blacks. In the scrum there was Willie Stileman, son of David of earlier years. Willie Stileman managed to play sixty-four times for Cambridge before he got a blue. Having done so, he moved over to Oxford, where he studied theology, and proceeded to get two more against his former university: the second time in the 1990 Varsity match, when Oxford, very much the underdogs, turned the tables decisively. Oxford's effort was all the more creditable as C.Sheasby, one of the more promising younger Harlequins, was playing for Cambridge: he played what is popularly known as 'a blinder of a game' and scored a try. David Cooke was captain this year, Richard Langhorn was already making his mark as a forward, and the two Evertons (Everton Weekes at number-eight and Everton Davis as wing three-quarter) showed devastating pace every time they touched the ball. One of the Quins young three-quarters, called W.Carling, appeared for England 'B': we all thought he might have a promising future.

Opposite: Dave Loveridge, the All Blacks scrum-half, who played for New Zealand over twenty times between 1978 and 1985. Like many of the Quins' New Zealand members, he made an enormous contribution to improving the playing and coaching standards of the club.

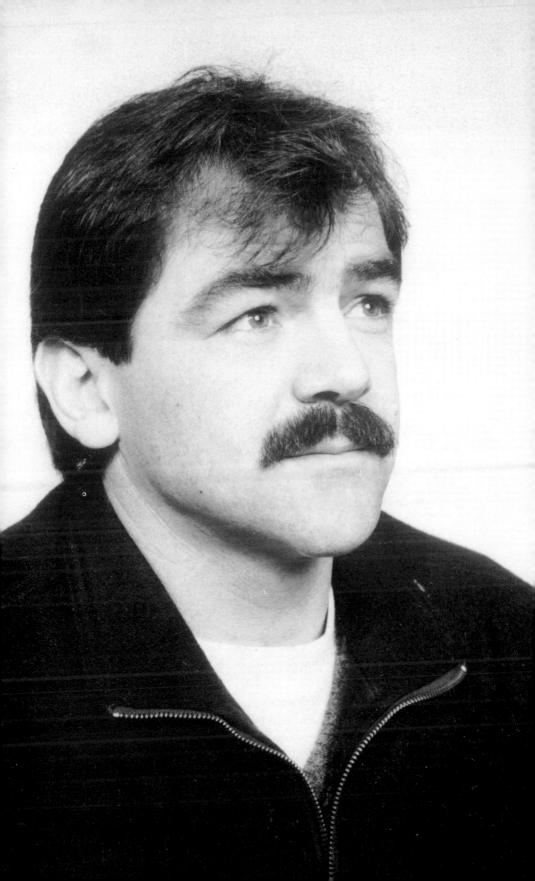

The results for the 1987-8 season showed a marginal improvement on previous years:

	Won	Lost	Drew	For	Agn
First XV	22	9	2	869	438
Wanderers	24	5	1	847	341
A1	15	6	1	No record of points.	
A2: No results recorded.					
Jaguars	23	7	2	611	226

Under-19s: No results available.

The most interesting and encouraging feature of this season was the change in attitude. All too often in the past the Quins had played well and won, or played well and then stupidly lost. This season they showed that they could play well and then, finding our opponents were a stiffer proposition than was at first thought, raise their game to the point of victory.

On paper, and in non-League or Cup matches, the Quins were their usual cheerful selves, winning against Blackheath, Richmond and Bedford with all their old panache. However, they put out a weakened side against Wasps and lost by one point, and could only draw with Gloucester in a match the Quins should have won. They were then outplayed by the Orrell steamroller and to their horror found themselves at the bottom of Division One of the League. There were, we knew, excellent clubs in Division Two, but the Quins had no wish to join them.

At that point the Quins decided that they would show the world they had steel in their backbones and fire in their bellies. They brushed aside the resolute players of Berry Hill and went on to dispose of Moseley, Waterloo and Coventry.

At the end of the season the Quins won the John Player Cup and came third in the League. The cover picture on *Rugby World* of the toothless (almost) John Olver, holding the Cup aloft, is one of the most dramatic in the Quins' 125-year history.

Nowadays, when so many people seem to play on their gum-shields like mouth organs (invariably picked up by the TV cameramen, who are probably all failed dentists), it made a change to see someone who cares less for his appearance than for results. This season was Olver's second as club captain, for he had taken over from David Cooke. Even for a hooker, John Oliver is rather small and light (height 5ft 9in, weight 13st 4lb) but in the rucks

Opposite: Participants of the Golden Oldies
match in 1987, with their cheerleaders in front.

and mauls he is more like an armour-piercing bullet than a slightly undersized forward.

To use the modern jargon, 'his commitment is total'. As so often happens, he coincided with another dedicated player, Brian Moore, who is also a formidable player in the open and John has therefore seen the recent full internationals from the excellent but frustrating viewpoint of the reserves' bench. John Olver was educated at Rossall in the spartan climate of the Lancashire coast, an experience he shared with Peter Winterbottom. He trained as a teacher at Borough Road College and is now on the staff of Northampton School. This, alas, has meant that he has left the Quins and joined Northampton. Although he is now approaching the 'veteran' mark (he was born in 1962), wise men seem to think he has a lot more rugger in him. He has captained the Quins and England 'B' and looks virtually indestructible.

The Wanderers continued to improve on their record, in spite of creating a different sort of record by using the total of eighty-one players. This was an astonishing performance, for at full-strength the Quins need only ninety players to occupy the entire playing complement of the club, including the Under-19s and the A2, which is usually noted more for its stamina in the bar than on the playing field. The A1 had a very good playing record. Amongst its regulars was Bill Cuthbertson who, a year or two earlier, had been a regular in the Scottish XV.

The Jaguars did very well too, although frequently having to supply players to the Wanderers. There was a growing air of confidence (though not of superiority) throughout all the teams this season and everyone felt that justice had been done when the Quins won both the John Player Cup and the Middlesex Sevens. And this in a season in which they had come within a whisker of being relegated.

Although tours are dealt with elsewhere in this book, we feel that a somewhat unorthodox one should be given a mention here. This was to British Columbia in May and consisted of a mixture of players from the Firsts, the Wanderers, and the Under-21s: it won three out of the four games.

Harlequinade, which had been asleep for seventeen years, was reawakened by Howell Thomas and has continued to enlighten and entertain us every since. In the first of the new issues, Howell Thomas, who was chairman of fund-raising, pointed out the vast change in finances since the Quins left Teddington.

At the end of that season (twenty-four years earlier) the club's income from all sources had been £6,000 and left them with a

Howell Thomas, the man who reawakened Harlequinade *to enlighten and entertain members of the Harlequin FC.*

profit of £331. In 1987, the Quins had an income of £113,000 and made a loss of £5,000. As income increased, so did the Quins' commitments and this made it urgently necessary to explore every possible means of fund-raising. The club aimed to attract as much sponsorship as they could and introduced match sponsorship which cost the sponsor £300 but gave him tickets, parking and entertainment facilities for up to thirty guests; on a lesser scale was ball sponsorship which cost £30 and gave the sponsor a mention in the programme. The Harlequin FC was also sponsored by certain companies, notably Whyte & Mackay Limited, Jaguar Cars Limited and, later, Red Star Parcels.

The finances of a Rugby Football club are like trying to fill a bath with a missing plug. You know that you can never stop the outflow, nor do you particularly want to, but preventing the bath running dry needs a variety of supplementary inflows apart from the two main ones of subscriptions and 'gates'.

The 1989-90 season results were as follows:

	Won	Lost	Drew	For	Agn
First XV	24	13	0	832	627
Wanderers	11	19	1	479	658
Jaguars	31	9	2	734	229

The results of the 'A's and Under-19s were not recorded, not because they were unsatisfactory but because the teams differed so greatly from match to match. During this season the Wanderers set up a new, and unwanted, record, by calling on over ninety players. This was an exceptionally bad season for injuries, but of course the Wanderers also bore the brunt of replacements for the Firsts and also county calls.

In view of the amount of talent available it may seem surprising that the First XV could lose as many as thirteen matches. However, it is considerably less surprising when one realises the extent of the calls made on the Quins' best players by international, divisional and county games, not to mention squad training sessions and injuries. There are, of course, times when even the most rugged player needs a rest. There used to be a popular word called 'stale' to describe a player who played so many hard games of rugger that he was beginning to lose all his fire, and just play mechanically. The word had dropped out of use, but the condition it describes is still with us.

Since the Quins adopted the squad system they have coped much better with team disruption and some of their results when they were very under-strength have been excellent. Very much depleted sides scored excellent victories against Richmond, Cardiff, Gosforth and Bristol. By the end of the season, fifty-nine players had appeared in the First XV. This dilution of talent is supportable when it is spread evenly over the season. A different pattern emerges when it happens all at once, for then the Quins may not be able to meet their commitments.

In December 1990, the Quins came to the crunch: they had thirty-eight players unavailable for one reason or another. Very reluctantly they had to cancel three first-team matches on consecutive Saturdays. Their opponents were disappointed but understanding. We, though, began to wonder whether the Quins had enough strength in depth.

This was a year in which the club did not win the Pilkington Cup, nor the League, but did win the Middlesex Sevens. In the circumstances they had a successful season and looked like having even better ones in the future now that Mike Davis had agreed to oversee and direct coaching throughout the club.

During the year the Quins increased their membership by over 260. Older members (who had not kept very closely in touch) were surprised to see that many women had now been elected full

Opposite: The 1990 Middlesex Sevens winners.

167

members. However, the Quins have not yet begun to run a Women's XV, unlike some of their ancient rivals (Wasps, Richmond) but they may well do so one day. For the moment women members are of the non-playing but hard-working variety.

Throughout their existence the Quins have relied on the distaff side to help them out in all the routine but vital domestic tasks of the club. Now the Quins have a chance to show their appreciation and give them the status they have earned.

For representative honours this had been an excellent year, as the following list shows:

British Lions: P.J.Ackford.

England: P.J.Ackford, W.D.C.Carling, A.Mullens, M.G.Skinner, P.J.Winterbottom.

England 'B': E.Davis, A.Mullens, C.J.Olver, D.Pears, M.G.Skinner.

England Under-21s: G.Thompson

England Colts: B.Short

England Under-18s: A.Compton, N.Brackett (captain).

England Students: A.Ward, B.Stanhope, J.Gibbon.

Barbarians: P.J.Ackford, W.D.C.Carling, N.Edwards, C.J.Olver, M.G.Skinner, P.Winterbottom, E.Davis, C.Sheasby, A.Thompson.

London Division: P.J.Ackford, W.D.C.Carling, P.Curtis, E.Davis, N.Edwards, A.Harriman, C.Luxton, M.G.Skinner.

Northern Division: D.Pears, P.Winterbottom.

U.A.U.: P.Thresher.

London Division Under-21s: G.Thompson (captain), M.Winn, P.Thresher, C.North.

The sad news this year was the death of Ken Chapman on 7 November 1989. As mentioned earlier, Ken had begun his services to the club as a three-quarter and was soon also carrying out the duties of secretary for the three 'A' XVs. In the second half of the 1930s he became captain and continued in that role when the club was restarted after 1945. Subsequently he was president of Middlesex and the Rugby Football Union. In all he was a member of the Quins for sixty years.

Ken was, of course, was a man renowned not for the offices he held but for what he did for them. As captain, secretary, trustee and president he added that vital bit extra. To the outside world his personality and wisdom created the impression that if he was a typical Harlequin, the club must be very good indeed. When he was afflicted with Parkinson's Disease he bore it with great courage, and made light of it with his philosophic humour. A friend recalls him saying, 'Let's go into the bar and spill some beer'. There aren't many people like Ken. On 23 February 1991, his portrait, painted by Michael Grimsdale, was unveiled by his son, Richard, at the Stoop at a reunion of his many old friends. It seemed as if he was there too.

Here and Now

THE 1990-91 season opened with a fixture against Belgium which resulted in an easy victory although the Quins' team was nowhere near full strength. Peter Winterbottom was club captain but as he was not available for this match, Stuart Thresher (vice-captain) took over the responsibility.

The Quins had four internationals playing that day, Jamie Salmon and Jason Leonard, Andy Mullins and Paul Ackford. Andy Mullins was the other prop forward and behind was the line-out specialist Paul Ackford. Brian Moore, the England hooker, had now joined the Quins from Nottingham but for this match was standing by as a replacement.

There were plenty of other good players in the Quins' side, particularly Richard Langhorn at number-eight, Adrian Thompson at fly-half and Robert Glenister at scrum-half. Later in the season the Quins would lose Adrian Thompson to Rosslyn Park.

During the 1980s, the Quins had had several exchanges of players with the Park and once, in the Middlesex Sevens, faced a Rosslyn Park VII which consisted mostly of former Harlequins.

At centre three-quarter was Will Carling, who had learnt his rugger at Sedbergh School and Durham University and had begun his career in the Army. He won his first cap in 1988, against France. In 1989 he was appointed captain of England (for three years) and he was the youngest player to hold that demanding position for fifty-seven years. With a height of 5ft 11in and a weight of 14st, he is able to stand up to the hard life of a centre three-quarter and to give as good as he gets. His great triumph this year was leading England to victory in the Grand Slam. His responsibilities have not been made easier by the relentless pressure on him by the media.

The fact that Carling gets a good supply of the ball is in great measure due to Paul Ackford, who with a height of 6ft 6in and a weight of 17st is a dominant figure in the line-out. Paul Ackford was educated at Plymouth College and Magdalene College, Cambridge, where he won a blue in 1979. In his early rugger career he played for Plymouth Albion and Rosslyn Park. In 1989 he went

Richard Langhorn, Paul Ackford, Micky Skinner and Andy Mullins in action.

to Australia with the British Lions and played in all three Tests. He has been a schoolmaster at Dulwich, but changed his career and joined the Metropolitan Police, in which he is now an inspector.

Soon to join Ackford as a lock forward was Troy Coker, an Australian who is studying law at Oxford. He is slightly larger than Ackford, being 6ft 7in tall and weighing 18st 8lb. He was educated at St Paul's, Brisbane, before coming to Oxford where he has won two blues: he had already been capped for Australia and will, no doubt, continue to add to his tally of international appearances. The fact that he is not only good in the line-out and the loose but also fast enough on his feet to have represented

Richard Langhorn and Troy Coker, the Australian studying law at Oxford.

Australia in the Hong Kong and Sydney seven-a-sides makes him somewhat exceptional for a man of his size.

Peter Winterbottom came to the Quins from Headingley, where he had won his first England cap in 1982. Before that he had been at school at Rossall, where he had been a contemporary of John Olver, who has now left the club for Northampton after captaining the Quins for three seasons.

In 1983, Winterbottom went to New Zealand with the British Lions and played in all four Tests. He began this season with thirty-seven England caps and looked set for many more. An open side flanker, 6ft tall and just under 14½st, Peter's tackling has been aptly described as 'terminal' to many a promising opposition movement. He began his working life as a farmer, but is now a Euro Bond dealer.

The first choice fly-half was also a northerner. David Peers comes from Workington, in the north of Cumbria, where he played for that formidable club, Aspatria, before moving to Sale. He joined the Quins in 1989 and won top points scored in that season with 208. He has played regularly for England 'B' and in both the Tests on the England tour of Argentina in 1990. He is understudy to Rob Andrew, the England fly-half.

One of the Quins' scrum-halves is Craig Luxton, a New Zealander of English ancestry. He came to England to see Europe, and stayed. He has now played for England 'B'. Before he arrived, the Quins' regular scrum-half was the Cambridge blue, Richard Moon, who gave the Quins valuable service, particularly in sevens, but has now moved to Rosslyn Park. However, another player to appear as scrum-half has been Rob Glenister, who is nearly as versatile as Roger Whyte used to be.

In the centre, next to Will Carling, the Quins now have Simon Halliday, who has played for England fifteen times, although most of the times as a member of Bath. However, he had been a Harlequin before his job took him to Bath, and now that it has brought him back to London he is with the club again, with many more caps in his sights.

As usual, the Quins have an excellent supply of talent in the three-quarter. One of the most consistent is Gavin Thompson, an England 'B' international. Gavin, who was educated at Whitgift, came from Rosslyn Park in 1989 and has the look of a future full international. In M.Wedderburn, M.Molyneux and E.Davis, the club has wings of the best Harlequin tradition, but the star of the show at the moment is undoubtedly Andy Harriman, formerly of Radley, and a Cambridge blue. He was capped for England in 1988 and, but for injury which kept him out of the game for a long period, must certainly have had more.

Harriman is the perfect example of the saying that you can do anything at rugger if you do it fast enough. His long stride makes the pitch look smaller than it is. The slightest hint of an opening in any direction and Harriman is through it.

The front row of the scrum is an all-international trio: Jason Leonard, already mentioned Brian Moore, who joined the Quins from Nottingham this year with a tally of twenty-nine England

Brian Moore, who joined the Quins from Nottingham with twenty-nine England caps already to his name.

caps and three appearances for the British Lions; and Andy Mullins. Chris Butcher, who often plays at number-eight, is already an international and Richard Langhorn looks a certainty as a future one. Of course, at the end of this season one or two of the old stalwarts may retire.

In these highly competitive times much thought must be given to the running of a club, if it is to be healthy and successful. It is not enough just to learn from the mistakes of the past and resolve not to repeat them: one needs an analysis which is not merely the negative one of avoiding errors, but a positive one of creating a club spirit and style which will carry on for the next two or three seasons.

One of those who made this positive analysis is Roger Looker, the Quins' present club chairman. Roger was recruited for the Harlequins in 1972 by Jay Gould, Howell Thomas and Ken Chapman, who had seen him playing for Old Alleynians against the Wanderers. The Old Alleynians (Dulwich College) have contributed many first-class players to the Harlequins in the past. Unfortunately, these days they are a shadow of their former greatness and when their president and captain were asked for permission to recruit Roger they readily agreed, realising that it would give him opportunities to develop as a player which Old Boy rugger could not provide.

Within weeks he was playing for the First XV and continued to do so for the next three years. He played for England Under-23s and for an England side against Fiji. Unfortunately the latter game did not, at that stage, command a full cap.

Looker's time with the Quins saw many changes. Playing at top level, in or on the fringe of international matches, makes enormous demands on a modern player's time and energy. Inevitably one's business or professional career suffers and family life comes a poor second. Looker was unwilling to jeopardise his business career by continuing to play on the off chance that Mike Burton or Fran Cotton, the current England prop forwards, might become unavailable and thus create a vacancy. Wisely he chose to retire.

When Roger Looker joined the club in 1972, it still contained such illustrious names as Hiller, Lloyd, Starmer-Smith, Wrench, Murray, Dixon, Rutter and Novak, but all were 'mature' and not always available every week. This was a period of explosive expansion in the national popularity of the game, but not a happy time for the Quins, with their former sources of supply — public schools, universities and the Services — becoming less fruitful. In the Midlands, the North, Wales and the West Country, many of the players came from a very different social background.

Roger Looker recalls: 'Earl Kirton was the captain in 1972-73 and he started to widen the base of the club's recruiting. His first capture was Terry Claxton, a lorry driver with a larger-than-life approach.

'Earl was, of course, captain, coach, head cook and bottlewasher all rolled into one. Like Dick Best, he also chose the side and made all the decisions. In those days the only other 'help' on the playing side was the admirable Tom Inwood, the team secretary and touch judge. Today, the First XV has two team secretaries, a pool of three physiotherapists and a boy who brings on the sand for the goal-kicker.

'Earl was succeeded by Mike Mason for one season and Nick Martin for two. Earl became the club's first coach. Nick Martin put in some startling performances on the field but lived and worked in Bury St Edmunds which, pre-M25, was virtually inaccessible from Twickenham and he rarely managed to get to training. Martin was succeeded by David Cooke, who played four times for England in the centre. When Earl returned to New Zealand, Stuart Winship coached the side: he was ex-Loughborough and full of technical knowledge.'

Looking back on the 1970s, Roger Looker feels that it was a decade of drift when 'we as a club were among many others who did not foresee how their comfortable existence and stable fixture list would soon be a thing of the past'.

In 1979, Looker was prevailed on by Jay Gould to take over as secretary of the club from John Seldon. Very reluctantly, he accepted. The fortunes of the Harlequins were at a low ebb. There was dissension among the higher management and the stock of players was 'pitiful'. Alexander was captain, the season started badly and got worse. Then Alexander departed to play Rugby League for Oldham. In his place Terry Claxton, 'the only experienced player of some standing in the game' was elected captain.

Looker continues: 'On Boxing Day the Quins had a piece of good fortune. Andy Haden came down to the club, having stayed over after the All Black tour. He was headed for Italy in the New Year but I was able to persuade him to play for us when matches did not clash with his commitments in Italy. This, he started to do. He seemed to enjoy himself and would play in England on Saturday and would then fly to Italy for a game there on Sunday. The effect of the presence of a world-class player on the Quins' motley band was amazing. We hardly lost a game for the rest of the season.

'We had not, however, been able to address the core problem: an appropriate playing structure and its own administration.

'During the summer of 1980 it was possible to take an objective view of the club, its shortcomngs, and its requirements. J.R.C.Young introduced Colin Herridge, who had been very successful as team secretary-manager of Surrey. Colin became the Quins' playing chairman and began to build up team administration by bringing in others, such as Sid Richardson who also had experience in this area.

'John Currie's appointment as chairman that summer was also important. Though neither an innovator nor an administrator, he was liked within the game and his legendary profile as a player was vital at a time when the Quins were not a force on the field.

'A year or so after my return from New York, I found myself chairman of the playing committee. It was immediately apparent to me that true professionalism in terms of preparation had now arrived. Players turned up for training fit, any player unfit (or late) was sent straight home and told to put in the basic groundwork before returning. Training sessions were carefully planned; it was not simply a question of making it up on the night. Practice sessions were clearly mapped out weeks in advance.

'Administration had moved ahead light years. If buses did not appear on time, if meals had not been pre-ordered, if we arrived at a hotel and found we did not have an adequate supply of balls for practice, Dick Best would have gone through the roof, so it never happened.

'We had two team secretaries just to make sure nothing went wrong. No one ever thought of not turning up to training. The medical requirement had also expanded. Physiotherapy was available at Stoop on training nights and a physio always travelled away. The result of this is that you rarely see anyone pull a hamstring or a calf muscle.

'Specialist athletic coaching is also now available to improve speed, and Mike Mein, who is coach at South London Harriers, also takes the warm-ups before training and matches.

'Best's years as a coach did not go totally smoothly. He was bedevilled by that old Harlequin bedfellow, inconsistency. His second season as coach (1987-88) started disastrously. By the beginning of February, the Quins had hardly won a League game and were staring relegation in the face.

'The rest of the story is now folklore but there were a few frights on the way. I remember a match at Coventry when the Quins could not afford to lose any more games. It was a procession of penalty-kicks and when we went into injury time we were behind. The awful drop into Division Two was there before us. Then Harriman and Thresher manufactured a try from nowhere, which was no mean feat in the Coventry mud . . .'

But, he went on to explain, it was still hard going; nobody was an automatic choice, at either international or club level. Nevertheless the team became bonded together (it remained unchanged for three months) and won the Pilkington Cup at the end of the 1987-88 season.

The lesson of the last two years seems to be that if it is difficult to get to the top, it is even more difficult to stay there. Usually one does not realise one's advantages until one has lost them. When the Quins played nearly all their First XV matches at Twickenham, the Rugby Football Union were their hosts and covered most of the outgoings. The Harlequins are still entitled to play thirteen matches a year at Twickenham, but in 1990-91 could only manage two, both being in September.

The Stoop has therefore become the Quins' principal ground.

John Moore-Gillon has taken over the responsibility of running the Stoop, and it is no minor task. Maximising revenue is a constant problem. When Looker was secretary, it was proposed to 'sack' National Car Parks, who were paying about £1,500 per annum for parking rights. The more timid members of the committee doubted whether the club could ever match this figure. Nevertheless, NCP were sent on their way and the club has profited considerably from its own administration of the parking facilities.

The situation today, now that the Harlequins are firmly established at the Stoop, is that there is the strengthening of a local association and mutual loyalties. Nevertheless, the Harlequins are in no way a restricted club. It is open to all and for the last 125 years has offered unmatched opportunities to talented players to develop their potential.

However, it is only one club and is powerless to influence trends in the game as a whole. We may not care for many modern developments but the Quins must make provision for them and accommodate changes, even if we don't all welcome them.

In the 1990-91 season it looked as if all the hard work put in behind the scenes was beginning to reap a handsome dividend. By mid-April 1991, the First XV had won twenty-two games and lost only nine. They were third in Division One of the Courage League and had reached the Final of the Pilkington Cup. The Wanderers had won fourteen games and lost seven. The Jaguars had won eighteen and lost six. The A1 had won nine and lost seven. The 'Gentlemen' had won fourteen and lost five and the Colts had won nine, lost five and also won the London Irish Colts Tournament. All this had been achieved without abandoning the Quins' style of play.

This season Harlequin teams were a pleasure to play in, and a joy to watch. The First had played very well apart from a bad dip over the Christmas period. The game against Bristol, a postponed League fixture, which eventually took place on Easter Saturday, had seen some strenuous work up front against a huge Bristol pack, and for some time the result had looked in the balance. Then the backs had really come into their own. Pears, a player of notable attacking potential, had given the three-quarters a quick supply of well-placed passes.

As mentioned before, Thresher had gathered a long kick-off from behind the Quins' line and started a movement which continued up to the half-way. Harriman drifted back and forth across the

Opposite: Will Carling, captain of England's 1991 'Grand Slam' winners. Carling, who learnt his rugger at Sedbergh School and Durham University, began his career in the Army. When he was appointed England captain in 1989, he was the youngest holder of that position for fifty-seven years.

pitch, never out of position when he was needed, but always using his electric acceleration to tear the opposition apart. Carling played the game of a lifetime, scoring three tries: he darted through like a salmon making a quick getaway through the reeds. Halliday was back in the form which had won him fifteen England caps.

The following week, the Quins met Nottingham in the semi-final of the Pilkington Cup. They went into the game against this greatly improved Midland side with considerable apprehension about the power of Simon Hodgkinson's boot, which had kicked England to victory in the Grand Slam championship. Fortunately for the Quins, who were missing Carling, injured in the match against Bristol, Hodgkinson was not quite as accurate as usual and the Quins won the game by a whisker (or at least an inspired try).

When the Quins met Moseley on the 13th, they still had a very faint chance of topping the League if all the other competitors at the top behaved uncharacteristically. But for Moseley, who had begun the season disastrously, it was a last chance to avoid relegation to Division Two. Moseley's forwards surprised their opponents but their back division was not as fast as the Quins, although they had one or two speedy runners.

As a result, the Quins beat them in a game which was played flat out until the final whistle. Afterwards, the Quins' team expressed considerable sympathy with Moseley, who had given them a most enjoyable game and were certainly of First Division quality. No doubt they'll soon be back.

That left the Harlequins with a non-League game against Rosslyn Park, a last League game against Gloucester away, and the Final of the Pilkington and the Middlesex Sevens. This was the third time the Quins had played Rosslyn Park this season, the first in the League, the second in the Pilkington Cup. The club fielded a strong team for this friendly and drew the game 19-19.

The following week the Quins drew at Gloucester for a League fixture. Winning or losing would make no difference to the Quins' final position in the League, which was third, so they sent the Wanderers to see how they would fare. In the event they did well to lose by only 38-19: Gloucester are a formidable proposition, whether home or away, but playing them on their home ground is a testing experience.

The Final of the Pilkington Cup was played at Twickenham

Opposite: Andy Mullins, the Quins' line-out specialist and one of four internationals who appeared against Belgium in the opening game of the 1990-91 season.

against Northampton on 4 May, before a crowd of 53,000. The previous week, Northampton had lost 48-0 to Rosslyn Park, but the bookmakers had not taken that result too seriously, even though the Quins were the clear favourites for the Cup.

Pears kicked-off into a wind which was blowing half a gale directly north-south down the pitch. This wind played no slight part in the game, for it made place-kicking very uncertain and also hampered the long, looping passes the Quins had used so effectively in earlier games. Towards half-time it began to veer north-east.

This stiff breeze really handicapped Northampton more than the Quins, for the local club knew all about the fickleness of the wind at Twickenham; it plays strange tricks as it comes around the tall stands and often has the touch flags flying in opposite directions.

But the biggest influence on this game was undoubtedly the marking and tackling of Northampton, who refused to be daunted by the fact that they were fielding only three internationals against the Quins' eleven. In the event, two of the Quins' outstanding players were neither of them internationals: Richard Langhorn and Everton Davis.

Langhorn, as usual, showed himself a master of the line-out, although no taller nor heavier than his Northampton opposites. And his try, late in the game, showed that his talents were not limited to the line-out. Although Harlequins took an early lead, Northampton fought back and within the dying minutes of the end of the game were leading 13-9.

With defeat now staring the Quins in the face, Carling slipped through the Northampton midfield defence and sent in Harriman for a try which needed all his pace as the defence closed in on him. That life-saver of a try meant that at full-time the two sides were equal and twenty minutes of extra-time had to be played to get a result.

This was going to be a test of ultimate fitness between two superbly trained teams. In the event, the decisive moment came as Pears kicked-off, a long low one into the wind, which dropped in the north-west corner, deep in the Northampton twenty-two. It was caught by their right wing but, as he prepared to kick safely into touch, a human bullet in the shape of Everton Davis came hurtling at him.

Davis did not reach the kicker but he charged down the kick

Opposite: Andy Harriman outpacing the
Northampton defence to score a vital try in the
1991 Pilkington Cup Final.

Numquam dormio, *the secret of success.*

which then rebounded into touch. A few minutes later there was a quick Harlequin heel and Simon Halliday slipped through the Northampton defence to score the vital try. Pears converted: it was 19-13 to the Harlequins.

Doggedly, Northampton battled back but in the second half of the extra period, Langhorn and Thresher between them contrived to send Glenister out for a try which Pears converted. The final score of 25-13 hardly demonstrates how narrow this victory had been.

An interesting feature of this game was that John Olver, the Northampton hooker, was the Quins' former captain. In a match of this heroic mould it is not fair to mention individuals without noting the total commitment of everyone in the team. The Quins' solid front row of Jason Leonard, Brian Moore and Andy Mullins wore down the opposition, Troy Coker was unlucky not to be awarded the try he appeared to have scored and Micky Skinner was in his usual form, which is high praise.

Team: S.Thresher; A.Harriman, W.Carling, S.Halliday, E.Davis; D.Pears, R.Glenister; J.Leonard, B.Moore, A.Mullins, T.Coker, P.Ackford, M.Skinner, P.Winterbottom, R.Langhorn.

Will Carling, the England captain, and Peter Winterbottom, club captain of the Harlequins, at the end of a long, hard, afternoon at Twickenham.

The spectators watching Peter Winterbottom brandish the Pilkington Cup after the game were unaware that the trophy itself had had some adventures and was lucky to be there at all. Colin Herridge recalls the celebrations after the previous victory in 1988.

'After the Cup Final, which was considered by journalists as the best ever (beating Bristol 28-22), I took charge of the Cup. A group of us ended up at closing time at "Albert Arms" in Esher and continued the Quins' celebrating with the Cup being handed around continually filled with bottles of champagne.

'Everything became hazy and it wasn't until three o'clock in the morning that I woke up in a cold sweat, trying desperately to remember where I had left the Cup. At nine o'clock in the morning, feeling like death, I was knocking on the door of the "Albert", asking if they had the Quins' Cup. Fortunately, the landlord had kept it safely after all the celebrations.'

The trophy, he discovered later, was not insured.

	Won	Lost	Drew	For	Agn
First XV	23	10	1	855	479
Wanderers	19	6	0	742	309
A1	19	6	0	647	292
A2 (Gentlemen)	19	7	1	573	333
Jaguars (Under-21)	26	6	0	756	296
Under-19	11	4	1	369	127

Tours and Sevens

NOWADAYS tours have become so popular and frequent that it is impossible to describe them all. There have already been a few references to certain tours earlier in this book. Until the middle of the present century, the highlight of the season for the First XV was the Easter tour in South Wales which, as we saw earlier, had a history stretching back to the early days of the club.

Although it was a holiday-like occasion, it involved some very tough matches against such doughty teams as Newport (sometimes), Swansea and Cardiff, and hospitality which at times was even more exhausting than the games. The Welsh hotels in which we stayed showed an amazing tolerance of some of the practical joking. Many proprietors in other parts of the country have now decided that the presence of a rugger team in the hotel is about as welcome as being struck by lightning.

Enjoyable though these excursions into South Wales were, they had a distinct disadvantage in that they clashed with the Barbarians tours. Harlequins were therefore almost precluded from membership of the illustrious Barbarians, who would hardly wish to elect non-playing members.

The Barbarians, of course, have other fixtures, one against the East Midlands, and another against Leicester on Boxing Day, as well as very occasional special ones against touring sides, but the club really comes into its own on its Easter tour. This explains why there are many less Barbarian Harlequins than there might have been. Nowadays, when the Quins have dropped our Easter tour, the position may change, but as the club also seems to be involved in so many other important fixtures around the Easter weekend, it may not.

One considerable disadvantage of Easter tours is that there is usually no first-class rugger to watch in London over the holiday period; therefore the disappearance of the Quins' Easter tour will be welcome to those of our spectators who decide to spend the holiday period in the capital.

Peter Woodruff recalls that Tom Bishop was the detonator for almost every practical joke on the Easter tour. The Pennard Golf

Club at Swansea became the virtual headquarters of the Harlequin team and although the presence of Bishop always ensured that the proceedings were boisterous to the point of being almost riotous, his personal popularity was so great that the Pennard golfers flocked to the club when it was known he was going to be present.

Wild ponies occasionally roamed around the golf course and one day Bishop issued a challenge that no one was man enough to catch one and ride it up to the clubhouse. The challenge was accepted by George Plumtree, who went out but instead of trying to lasso a wild pony, borrowed a huge mare from a nearby farm. The cheer which greeted the otherwise docile animal so unsettled it that it demolished the verandah before it calmed down. Alarmed bridge players and other elderly members appeared from remote corners of the club with considerable tut-tutting, but Bishop promptly diverted the club kitty to buying them all drinks and general goodwill soon prevailed.

Bishop usually arrived in a large open Vauxhall tourer, with a dicky seat, which he would lend to anyone on condition that they wore a top hat and tail coat and blew at intervals on the post horn, all of which were carried in the car. On one occasion the car and three passengers decided to call at a large house where one of them, a future distinguished airman, had promised they would be welcome for tea. Unfortunately the map reference had been misread and the party drew up outside a girls' school. Bishop's party was so persuasive that they really had been invited to tea that eventually they were. However, having made their point they politely declined and departed.

At one of the hotels at which the team stayed there was a long dining table, and as there were two other Rugby Football teams in residence, Bishop persuaded the manager that it would be very amusing if they held a competition to run up to the table, dive down it, and then walk away with a bottle which had been placed at the far end. Starting signals were given by small fireworks which Bishop, by chance, happened to have in his pocket.

The Harlequins were consistently victorious but, as the manager ruefully discovered, this was not the best treatment for the surface of a highly-polished table. However, after a few drinks with Bishop he decided it had all been grand fun even though he stipulated that they would have to find another hotel for the following year's tour.

Bishop's practical jokes, though alarming, never did any physical damage to anyone but fellow Harlequins, even though breakages of furniture and glass sometimes cost the club funds a sizeable sum in compensation. One of his more spectacular feats was to spill a few drops of lighter fuel (bottles of which stood on the bar for the convenience of smokers) and then accidentally light it. This gave those leaning on the bar a memorable, although temporary, experience. On one occasion he slightly overdid it and had to smother the flames with an overcoat lying on a chair nearby. To his chagrin he then found it was his own, and none the better for it.

To those who might enquire what is the difference between this sort of behaviour and yobbo hooliganism, there is a clear answer. During this period of high-spirited jollity, the club went out and played hard and entertaining Rugby Football, and gave enjoyment to many thousands of spectators. The hotels knew very well what might be in prospect when they booked in an entire Rugby Football team and its administration, and adjusted their prices accordingly. Bar sales shot up to record heights, for the presence of the club in the hotel drew in large numbers of other drinkers, anxious to see these 'foreigners' at close quarters.

Some of the escapades became legends and furnished a topic of bar conversation for years to come. The presence of Rugby Footballers was welcomed in the towns, in sharp contrast to the dread and loathing aroused by present-day mindless drunkenness.

The Easter visits to Wales were more light-hearted than many of our other tours have been, as when travelling abroad we were very conscious of our semi-ambassadorial status. The Quins' earlier overseas fixtures with the Racing Club de France have already been mentioned, as have their visits to Germany. In 1956 there was the visit to Romania; and in 1961 the Quins were the first overseas club to visit East Africa. In 1966 they inaugurated club tours to South Africa.

In 1964, the Harlequins visited Italy and defeated their national team 30-17.

For approximately fifty years of the Quins' existence, tours were a perk of the First XV. However, since those days the rest of the club has got in on the act. The Wanderers were soon making their way to Germany, Belgium and Ireland; then Howell Thomas decided that the south-west corner of France, a Rugby Football stronghold, would benefit from the club's presence and organised a series of matches based first on St Jean de Luz and later Toulouse.

Howell fondly imagines that in 1992 he will be able to make a substantial reduction in his commitment to club activities: he could be mistaken. Over the last forty years he has shouldered the burden of endless time-consuming, and often frustrating, tasks,

The 1950 Easter tour party pictured at Swansea. A.D.Stoop is centre of the seated row. On his right is J.R.C.Matthews, on his left M.J.Daly and D.K.Brooks.

such as being a team manager, team secretary, fixture secretary, committee man, organiser of special occasions, chairman of fund-raising, and representative of the club on the RFU outside sub-committees.

Through all that time he has applied an enormous amount of invaluable creative thought to the club activities. He nursemaided the Wanderers for the first ten years of its semi-independent existence. He began the club magazine *Harlequinade*, edited it from May 1960 to February 1970; then, after he had taken a breather, (during which no one else was willing or able to carry out the task) revived it in 1987 and still edits it today. Well aware that the club is always short of money, he was the originator, with fellow members Walter Hayes and John Southgate, of a car raffle which raised £29,000. Perhaps his most remarkable contribution was to launch the Harlequin Sevens.

Creative thought is needed in every part of a Rugby Football club and never more than in the improvement of finances. Howell

The 1961 tour party in Kenya, looking very smart in their blazers.

had observed the enormous success of the Middlesex Sevens and its earning capacity and noted that this and almost every seven-a-side competiton took place at the *end* of the season. A considerable source of enjoyment and revenue was therefore lying untapped at the beginning of the season, before serious matches began. In consequence, invitations were issued to various clubs, usually those, like Melrose and Bridgend, which had been successful in other parts of Britain. It was to be hoped that the Quins might win the competition more often than their guests, without actually monopolising it.

The very first tournament took place on 7 September 1968 and was won 21-13 by Cardiff, who defeated the Harlequins in the Final. The other teams who took part were Bath, Llanelli, North of Ireland, Loughborough College, Blackheath and Melrose. Melrose were beaten 9-8 by Blackheath in the main competition but won the Plate by beating North of Ireland.

The hosts were glad that Melrose did not depart empty-handed, for it was on their ground, 'Greenyards', that seven-a-sides had begun in 1882; the tournament was the brainchild of a local butcher

The 'jersey game' of 1965. Alan Soutar, the Australian Harlequins captain, receives the jersey from the Tasmanian Harlequins skipper (see page 203).

as a means of raising money for the club. The Melrose club dates back to 1877; it is said that it was founded by three Yorkshiremen who were in the district to learn the tweed trade, but no self-respecting Scotsman can be expected to believe that such a flagship of Scottish Rugby Football can have been started by Sassenachs.

In the following years many clubs have taken part in the Harlequins' Invitation Sevens: Bridgend, Moseley, Gloucester, Blackrock, Hawick, Stade Toulousain, Saracens, Rovigo (Italy), Paris University, Orrell, Northampton, Neath, St Luke's, Dublin Wanderers and Cambridge University have all been their guests.

Organising a sevens is enormously complicated and requires large numbers of helpers. Bright ideas for making this a fun day came in from all sides: some unknown genius arranged that attractive girl friends and daughters should sell programmes and raffle tickets. They were dressed in Harlequin jerseys with skirts so short that it appeared to the uninitiated (and optimistic) that the Quins jerseys were all that they were wearing.

Like the Middlesex Sevens, this was a charitable venture, although the spin-off would be the publicity it would give the club. Soon the Quins were working in close co-operation with the Lord's Taverners and in consequence elected some distinguished non-playing members. The Lord's Taverners, with whom the Harlequins established the link in 1981, had been formed in 1950 with the aim of playing and organising cricket matches in aid of charity. Its members were mostly actors, were all cricket enthusiasts and keen patrons of the Tavern at Lords.

Sir Denis Thatcher and Sir Brian Rix at the Stoop for the presentation of a New Horizons coach.

Their fund-raising was phenomenally successful. 'New Horizon' coaches were given to homes for handicapped children, a golf course was established for children in wheelchairs, substantial contributions were made to Normansfield to enable disabled children to ride, and a gymnasium equipped for the blind was provided for Dorton House, amongst other deserving causes. Youth cricket was also a major beneficiary.

The link with the Lord's Taverners had been established in 1981, when a sub-committee, consisting of Howell Thomas, Denis Culver,

Rodney Pollard and Gordon Provan, had agreed that, whilst the Quins would continue to organise the tournament, the Taverners would receive a guaranteed sum of money plus a share of the profits: in return they would help sell and support the event. Tony Swainson, director of the Taverners, then suggested an eve-of-tournament dinner, on the lines of the eve-of-Test Match dinners in cricket.

Soon afterwards, private hospitality tents were introduced and in 1990 a full house of thirty-seven tents was achieved. Various sponsors were recruited, beginning with Whyte & Mackay, and later including Akai, BMW, Jaguar Cars (1984-90). Jaguar also sponsored the Quins' under-21 team, which became known as the Jaguars. Vauxhall Motors have now taken over the sponsorship of both the Sevens and the Jaguars from 1991.

The original ladies' committee, which looked after catering, was Suzanne Roberts (chairman), Pat Hollins, Pat Orr, Susan Seldon and Norma Thomas. After four years, Pat Hollins succeeded Suzanne Roberts as chairman. Later recruits to the 'team' were Peggy Todman, Pat Parker, Barbara Pragnell, Pam Ashworth, Jean White and Susie Moore-Gillon.

Since linking up with the Quins for the Sevens, the Lord's Taverners have received £66,000 from the tournament plus £10,000 from the blanket collection. In addition, £6,500 was raised for charity from the eve-of-sevens dinner. In the twenty-three years since this tournament began, the Harlequins have benefited by over £150,000.

The Wavell Wakefield Trophy, for the winners, was not won

The Wavell Wakefield Trophy for the Harlequins Invitation Sevens. Each member of the winning team receives an engraved cut-glass tankard.

Lord Wakefield presents the Wavell Wakefield Trophy to Cardiff, the first winners of the Invitation Sevens, at the Stoop in 1968.

by the Harlequins for sixteen years until 1983. It was lost to Bridgend the next year (1984) but won again in 1985 and 1986. Wakefield won it in 1987, Llanelli in 1988, Bridgend in 1989 and Harlequins once more in 1990.

The Middlesex Sevens, which now has an attendance rivalling that of international matches, began in 1926 and for the first four years of its existence was won by Harlequins. W.W.Wakefield played in all four winning teams. Harlequins did not win again till 1933, when they trounced Wasps 23-0. J.C.Gibbs, who had played in

A very distinguished Quins team, winners of the 1926 Middlesex Sevens. Back row (left to right): J.R.B.Worton, W.F.Browne, J.S.Chick, J.C.Gibbs. Front row: W.W.Wakefield, V.S.Davies (captain), R.H.Hamilton-Wickes.

1926 and 1928, turned out again for this game in 1933. The Barbarians won in 1934, but the Harlequins were back in 1935.

From 1935, the Middlesex Sevens were a bleak hunting ground for the Quins. They reached the Final in 1948 but then lost 14-5 to Wasps. Not until 1967, when they defeated Richmond 14-11, did Harlequins carry off the trophy again.

Their next appearance in the Final was 1971, but it resulted in a defeat by London Welsh, 18-9. The year 1976 saw another appearance in the Final but this time the Quins suffered a narrow defeat of 21-20 at the hands Loughborough College. Two years later seemed to herald a brighter dawn, when the Harlequins defeated Rosslyn Park 40-12, but it was the prelude to seven lean years.

The year 1986 saw a revival in the defeat of Nottingham by 18-10. This was the start of a five-year winning sequence, which was only broken in 1991, when London Scottish won a tense Final

Above: Peter Winterbottom receiving the Russell Cargill Cup from Michael Christie, the Middlesex president, in 1990. Opposite: Andy Dent receives congratulations (and the Middlesex Sevens trophy) from P.G.Yarranton.

by 20-16. An irony of that year was that Harlequins I had to defeat Harlequins II in order to reach the Final.

However, this still left the Harlequins with the longest winning sequence in the Middlesex Sevens and the greatest number of wins in the tournament since it began.

Now and Then

IN THE distant past, Rugby Footballers were almost anonymous figures, known only by their names and initials. Even the great Adrian was A.D.Stoop. Until the last few decades it seemed to be assumed that if players had christian names they very correctly kept quiet about them.

Initials, of course, sometimes acquired a quality of their own, particularly if they spelt something. This was particularly noticeable at cricket where M.C.Cowdrey also signified M.C.C. and W.G.Grace and J.B.Hobbs seemed to imply they would be difficult to dislodge once they reached the crease. K.H.Chapman, D.F.B.Wrench, J.G.Willcox and C.M.Payne had initials which suggested that their owners were not men who would easily be brushed aside.

In recent times initials have tended to give way to first names. English clubs do not have the same trouble that Welsh teams encounter: Williams, Evans, Rees, etc, but when the Quins had two Cookes, both called David, both English internationals, and both captains of the club, it was not easy to know which one was being referred to.

Nowadays the ever-dominant media have exposed us to what is known as the cult of personality. We may deplore it but we can't ignore it. And, of course, it has its merits. it is interesting to know that Humphrey Tilling was not merely a talented three-quarter but also a brilliant actor and impersonator. R.W.D.Marques, P.R.Y.Anderson, R.H.C.Page and J.S.M.Scott were also good enough sailors to compete in the America's Cup. Richard Langhorn, the Quins' 6ft 6in, 16st 7lb, number-eight, was educated in both Australia and England (Sevenoaks) and is also a very competent basketball player.

Joe McPartlin, Oxford blue and Scotland international, is renowned for his wit. Among the remarks he is alleged to have made when watching matches is: 'I've seen better centres in a box of Black Magic chocolates'. To a fellow Harlequin in his own playing days he remarked: 'With your speed and my brains we could make quite a good centre between us'. He recalls that once when he was playing fly-half for the Harlequins the scrum-half was injured and a forward (Marriot) had to deputise. After the game McPartlin observed: 'I don't mind getting the ball along the ground all the time, or even having to fall on it, but when I did go down it was always Marriot who was first to kick me in the back'.

Anyone who bought a programme for the Oxford v Cambridge match used to look first to see whether McPartlin had contributed one of his witty articles and secondly who was playing. It was a matter of getting one's priorities right.

Grahame Murray joined the Harlequins when still a schoolboy, admittedly rather a large one, at Wrekin. Then came National Service and Oxford, where he got a blue in his third year. He was then offered Scotland and England trials on the same day, having a dual qualification. After much thought he accepted the England offer. To his delight he was summoned to Twickenham to play against Wales but the selectors had changed their mind by the time he arrived and had put in an older prop forward. His chance never came again. He was First XV secretary in 1964 and club captain in 1965, and went on tour to South Africa in 1966. The Harlequins won three matches, lost two and drew one. 'David Brooks as manager was a tower of strength and "won" all his matches in the bar.'

Murray recalled that Bob Hiller introduced into the team 'that little element of discipline and training that had been lacking before. Those who think Dick Best tough never trained under Bob.'

After fifteen seasons as a player Murray turned to coaching, having been on the Rugby Union coaching course at Lilleshall in 1972. He also began turning out for the Quins junior sides. In 1987 he played in the Golden Oldies festival at Twickenham. Top hats and tails were borrowed from Moss Bros to wear on the march past. 'We played a Yugoslavian side, Zrelo Doba, who were doing rather well until we brought on the champagne at half-time.' For the last two years he has been joint chairman of the playing committee with Bob Hiller.

Murray emphasises that neither he nor anyone else would be able to play and then administer as he has done without the unflinching support of their wives. Annie Brooks and Norma Howell are particularly notable examples. His own wife, Jean, was pregnant when he went on the South African tour and if this was not enough to contend with had to run the family printing business as well.

As we have said earlier, the club thrives not merely because Harlequins play hard and devote long hours to administration, but because their wives make it possible for them to do so. Doubtless it is the same in many other clubs.

D.H. 'David' Cooke (a forward) was another long-serving member of the club. He joined at the age of eighteen, after learning his rugger at Haileybury, and played his first game for the First XV against Rosslyn Park: he was carried off at half-time with torn knee ligaments. He remembers being called off the field in a morning game against the Army and told he was to play against Romania that afternoon. At first he thought it must be a practical joke.

In 1981 he played against Wales, Scotland, Ireland and France, in 1984 against Ireland and in 1985 against Romania, France, Scotland, Ireland, Wales and New Zealand twice. He captained Middlesex when they won the County Championship in 1985 and was captain of the Harlequins from 1983 to 1987. He played his last game for the Quins in 1987, against Llanelli.

J.S.M. 'John' Scott joined the club after leaving Oxford, where he had won two blues and an England cap in 1958. His first games for the Quins were at Teddington, an open and windswept ground. As full-backs hate grounds which are very much exposed to the wind, Scott decided to plant trees whenever he went. He was also very active on the social side, organising fund-raising events such as dinners and dances. The Teddington clubhouse was a barn-like, inhospitable structure at that time and to make it suitable for social activities, a lot of hard work was required from a team of volunteers led by David Marques.

Having put in so much time improving Teddington, Scott was appalled when the club meekly sold the freehold on moving to the Stoop. Scott thinks that both as a player and a personality, Ricky Bartlett was the person who has done more for the Quins than perhaps anyone, not excepting the early pioneers. He mentions that Ricky's son, Harry, was a great supporter of the Wanderers and 'A' XVs in the 1980s and in 1982, as a Royal Marine, was one of the first ashore for the march to Goose Green in the Falklands.

Pat Cleaver recalled the Teddington ground in the early Fifties, before it had been improved. Excellent though the rugger was which took place there, there were seldom more than half a dozen spectators. This seemed to surprise visiting teams such as Cardiff or Swansea, who were accustomed to playing to several thousand. Cleaver has vivid memories of sharing a 3-litre Lagonda (a luxurious, elegant sports car) with Ricky Bartlett, the arrangement being that Cleaver would have the car during the Cambridge term and Bartlett would have it during the vacation. This worked reasonably well except that at the end of the vacs, Ricky would bring the car back, limping on two of its six cylinders, and 'it would take just about the whole term to get it right again'. Eventually they sold it because it was too expensive to run.

Vintage cars and the Harlequins seemed to go together in the Fifties. Cleaver borrowed a Railton 'Straight Eight' from Geoff Bulter to drive to Cornwall, for whom he was playing in a County Championship match. It was a very cold day, there was no heater in the car, but the cooling system boiled at intervals and had to be left to cool. After hitting a lump of frozen snow outside Exeter, it skidded into the ditch. With the help of passers-by it was hauled back on to the road and completed the journey. As the return journey was over 500 miles and the Railton's eight cylinders had an inordinate thirst for petrol, the reaction of the Cornwall committee when the expenses claim came in was dramatic. However, they paid up.

'In the Fifties,' wrote Cleaver, 'training was very sparse and there is little doubt that few of us would make the First XV at current levels of fitness and skill. Despite having a strong pack, we played an open game. The most important aspect was the immense enjoyment derived from playing the game, and I only hope that enjoyment will continue into the foreseeable future and beyond. In my view it stands a far greater chance of doing so if the game retains its amateur status.'

John Gronow played for the Quins for twenty-five seasons, beginning in 1964. Asked whether he was related to Captain Gronow, a veteran of Waterloo and other battles and the author of many witty observations on the society of his day, John Gronow answered: 'My late father, who was an eccentric alcoholic sportsman, always claimed we were related, but frankly I doubt it.

'He also claimed we were related to Ben Gronow, a Welsh international, who created history (it is alleged) when he kicked-off in the first Rugby Union international at Twickenham. He joined Huddersfield Rugby League Club in 1910 so we don't talk about him.'

For the first eight years of his playing career, John Gronow was officially the scrum-half of the Wanderers, but as Starmer-Smith, the First XV scrum.half, was often unavailable, Gronow was frequently promoted. As a result he managed to play against such legendary figures as Gareth Edwards and Chris Laidlaw.

'However if I had to pick the most satisfying game it would probably be the win against Llanelli at Stradey Park by 15-11 in February 1971. As it was the day of the English County Final, we were fielding a Wanderers back division; nevertheless we became the only English side to win at Stradey Park that season.

'The previous September, Llanelli had beaten us 56-5 at Twickenham. We were 11 points down at half-time, then Peter Carroll trundled over in the corner for a try and that gave us great confidence as we thought that if Peter can score a try anyone can. There was no stopping us after that, despite the presence of Phil Bennet, Delme Thomas, Barrie Llewellyn and Derek Quinell in the Llanelli team.

'Anyway, the journey back was very relaxing, although Tommy Thomas thought the bill of £96 for champagne might be difficult to get approved. The team that day was: Peter Carroll, Paul Grant, John Gibbs (son of the geat J.C.Gibbs), Dave Coley, Nigel Lewis, Earl Kirton, John Gronow, Bryce Wilson, Gerry Miller, Stack Stevens, Keith Jones, Nick Martin, Mike Mason, Peter Dixon and Charlie Bale. A scrum-half always felt confident with the likes of Nick Martin, Stack Stevens and Peter Dixon in front of him.'

Seven of that team played in Gronow's 'memorial' game in 1990 to celebrate his twenty-five years of playing for the club. As he said, 'Memories fade but friendships last'.

Older members will have noted that a new team has now appeared on the scene, 'The Harlequin Gentlemen'. This is really the old 'A2', in which the more mature members play out their declining years. The 'Gentleman' are determined to prove that Rugby Football is not a game for young men only. They are equally determined to show that on and off the field rugger is fun, a fact which tends to be obscured in these very competitive days.

The Gentlemen are well-qualified to debate such important topics as who was the oldest, heaviest, or youngest member ever to have played for the club. In such conversations one is likely to disentangle a true story from mere hearsay. For example, in one of his books the late Richard Burton (the actor) tells a story of a match between two teams in Wales. 'Suddenly a forward leapt out of the scrum clutching his ear which was bleeding profusely. The referee blew a shrill blast and pointed to another hulking forward. "You can't blame me ref," said the man indignantly. "My teeth are in the trainer's pocket." '

In fact it happened when the Wanderers were playing in Wales. The suspect was the Welsh hooker, who was almost entirely bald. As he spluttered indignantly to declare his innocence, his captain intervened. 'Dai can't talk properly without his teeth and he always leaves them in the changing rooms. Shall I go and get them and give him a chance to explain himself?'

Most of the Quins members are keen cricketers and golfers. Cricket has already been mentioned. Golf has provided some remarkable entertainment on tours, on golf days, and in conjunction with the Women's Professional Golf Association. In consequence, in 1990 the Quins launched the Harlequin Golf Society. The first meeting was held at Harewood Down Golf Club in the Chilterns on 21 March 1990.

It was a typical Harlequin occasion, bags of fun and enthusasm, with (very) occasional glimpses of brilliance. The club thrives, and with a subscription of £10 per annum is clearly within the reach of the most impecunious members.

The word 'Harlequin' has now become so much a symbol of an open, attacking, style of play that it has been adopted by many junior clubs in Britain, who simply tack the word 'Harlequin' on to their regional name. However, on a larger scale, it is a matter of considerable pride that there are official overseas Harlequin clubs. These are in South Africa, Australia, Tasmania, New Zealand, Kenya and the USA. The oldest is the Harlequin Club of Pretoria, South Africa, although this resembles our Barbarians more closely than it does an ordinary club.

The Pretoria Harlequins had begun as the Civil Service Club in 1902, but when it became apparent that there were not enough civil servants to make the club viable, it had to look elsewhere. In 1906 it extended its membership beyond the Civil Service and wrote to the Quins' committee to ask to use the club's name and colours. Permission was readily granted. The 'new 'club flourished and at one point in its history ran seven teams. It has produced an impressive number of internationals and has won many trophies. Inevitably, it has strong cricket and golf sections.

The Australian Harlequins club was founded in 1928 in Melbourne, Victoria. It was at first restricted to players who had been born in the British Isles but now membership is open to all. It has an excellent record in inter-club matches.

The Tasmanian Harlequin FC dates from 1933 and is based on Hobart. It runs several successful XVs and since 1948 has had an annual fixture with the Australian Harlequins, for which a silver tankard and an ancient jersey is the trophy. The 'cup' match takes place alternately in Melboune and Hobart: the towns are a mere 500 miles apart.

The New Zealand Harlequin FC was founded in 1938. It is based in Hamilton, Waikato, New Zealand. It has made a creditable beginning before it had to go into abeyance on the outbreak of World War Two; it was revived again in 1946. Membership is restricted to ex-Waikato (County) representatives, All Blacks or members of the New Zealand Services team, and Kiwis and certain invited players. With this membership it is not surprising that it puts some formidable teams on to the field.

The Kenya Harlequin FC was founded at Nairobi in 1952 and runs several teams. Many of its fixtures involve travelling 200 miles, which is rather different from the Quins' experience of being able to play many of their games without moving out of London. When the Quins toured East Africa in 1961, the Kenya Harlequins had made admirable arrangements for the tour; this included bringing up the Pretoria Harlequins, who then played their first-ever match against the Kenya Harlequins. It was a close contest which the home team narrowly won.

The American Harlequins FC is based on Dallas, Texas. Our latest report from them indicates that they are flourishing and winning plenty of matches.

A club of a different sort, and much nearer home, is the Harlequin Supporters' Club. The club was founded in April 1989 and since then its growth has been meteoric. A mere two years old, the membership now stands at 260. It came into existence because a few creative thinkers, notably Lee Paterson, Malcolm Coombs, Steve Hancock, Ray McCormack, Andy Stewart and Trevor Bond decided that many of the club's loyal supporters would appreciate having an organisation in which they could discuss games, promote social activities and travel as a group to away matches.

Despite the brilliant, spectacular Rugby Football which the Quins have played for many years, the club's home 'gates' have never been as good as they should have been, and for away games support has often been abysmal. Within a year, the 'new club' was providing much valued support, home and away, and had its own special tie, car stickers and even Harlequin ballpoint pens.

In addition, it was establishing links with other supporters' clubs throughout the country, co-ordinating applications for tickets for representative games, and had taken the first steps to organising an expedition overseas, possibly to New Zealand in 1993 for the British Lions tour. A notable social occasion was the Riverboat Shuffle when 100 members embarked on the 'Yarmouth Belle' on 13 September 1990 at Kingston-on-Thames and ate and drank, and danced and talked for the next four hours.

The Supporters' Club is obviously going to have a vigorous and enterprising future. It has already shown that it can offer valuable support to the main club by boosting attendance at both home and away games. Rugby Football is a sociable game but sadly this sociable side is usually limited to the playing members. In the past, loyal supporters have often gained the impression that they were tolerated rather than welcomed. No longer will this be so. The main club has given full co-operation to the supporters, making a loan for certain initial purchases, and arranging that current First XV players should attend some of the social occasions.

Some spectators prefer to be loners and watch games in solitary isolation, and everybody respects their right to do so: however, there are large numbers who are united by enthusiasm for the Harlequins, for the game and sociable activities. The Supporters' Club is just what was needed and will undoubtedly be of great benefit to the club and many other people too.

Everyone who watches a game of Rugby Football will have noticed that more often than not the ball bears the words 'Gilbert' and 'Match'. As the Harlequins have been using Gilbert balls for the last 125 years, it seems appropriate to find out a little more about their history. The present managing director of the company, readers will be interested to know, is Rodney Webb, the former Coventry and England wing three-quarter. The original manufacturer was William Gilbert, one of the boot and shoe makers to Rugby School in 1851. (He also used to make catapults which were then called 'tweakers': they were, of course, forbidden by the school authorities.) The former factory, at 5 St Matthew's Street (opposite Rugby School) is now a free-entrance museum, full of balls, bladders and much other fascinating Rugby Football memorabilia.

William Gilbert had prodigious lungs and as there were no pumps in his day could blow up the largest balls tight: the bladder was, quite literally, a pig's bladder. The practice seemed to do him good, for he lived to the age of 78, which was considerably more than the average life expectancy of his day. Gilbert's Rugby balls were so much better than any rival product that soon he was exporting them to Australia and New Zealand. The balls did not necessarily have to be oval, but that shape made them particularly suitable for the type of football played at Rugby, in which scores could only be made by kicking over the bar, not under it, and the ball was passed from hand to hand.

Apparently the balls were larger and more rounded than modern ones and kicks of seventy yards were not uncommon. Rubber bladders came in early in the 1870s and pumps came in t the same time. This made a pleasant change from the unhygienic 'green' bladders which could only be inflated by pushing the stem of a clay pipe into the opening. Size was not standardized until 1892.

In 1923, a centenary match was played on the Rugby School Close (commemorating William Webb Ellis' effort in running with the ball). W.W.Wakefield collected the two balls to be used in the match, and specified how tightly they should be inflated. (Mr Jiggle was by now the expert at inflation in Gilberts, though not with his lungs.) The match was England and Wales versus Scotland and Ireland. In addition to Wakefield, two other Harlequins, W.J.A.Davies and A.L.Gracie, were playing. Whenever touring sides visit this country, they always visit Rugby and walk on the close, where the game began.

In the Sixties, Gilberts went into decline, mainly because it had refused to move with the times and bring in synthetic balls or up-to-date technology. It was sold and appeared to have an uncertain future. However, in 1981 it was sold again, this time to Rodney Webb Sports Limited, who revitalised it; now, with a combination of the old and new, it is in a stronger position than ever. So great is the demand for Gilbert balls that ten weeks is now quoted as the normal delivery time.

However, the appeal of Gilbert Rugby balls to modern players is not merely sentimental. Most present-day players consider that they are easier to kick and handle than rival products. Old William Gilbert would be proud of that.

If the recipe for success is to combine the best of the old with the best of the new, the story of the Harlequin Football Club over the last 125 years is a good example of putting that into practice. The club has adjusted to the fierce heat of modern competition without abandoning the style of play which made the Quins famous. Their tradition is to look forward, not backwards: nobody sits complacently and thinks that we can rest on our laurels. On the field of play, the Quins try out new tactics and if they do not work, discard them and try fresh ones.

Behind the scenes they are always on the look-out for new talent and means of developing it. The Harlequins will always need more money because they believe the best policy with money is to make it and spend it rather than scrape and save with dubious economies. Two years ago, the club launched the Harlequin Shop, managed by Hugh Forbes, voluntarily of course. It flourishes and meets a long-felt need. The Stoop, that former council rubbish dump, with all the glamour of once housing a sewage works, is now one of the most attractive grounds in the country: John Moore-Gillon and his devoted team have seen to that.

Peter Forbes, chairman of the finance committee (and brother of Hugh), intends that its future will be more impressive than its past.

There are, of course, many Harlequins who have given long and devoted service to the club whose names do not appear in this book. The need to time publication for the 125th anniversary has made it impossible to contact all the 1,500 members of the club, but that does not mean that its debt to them is any the less.

We are doing very well in the Harlequins at the moment but we know that we must always be looking creatively at the future. We are proud to be the symbol of all that is good in the Rugby Football game. But complacency and inertia could wreck us. The Greeks had a word for it: 'hubris', the chastisement for those who become too pleased with themselves and indulge in mutual congratulations. Nobody who is mentioned in this book expects to be carried shoulder-high off the field. Harlequin football is a fifteen-man game and we all know that the man who scores a try or kicks a goal is only one of the team. We are lucky to be Harlequins, however good or bad we are as players. We owe a lot to our friends and supporters, and we are aware that we shall be popular as long as we are modest in success and gracious in defeat. In the future, as in the past, membership of the Harlequin Football Club must mean you are dedicated, unselfish, loyal, modest and friendly. It is as simple as that.

Injury Time

W HEN full time has been reached and the referee is keeping a close eye on his watch, some unexpected talent may emerge in the extra minutes allowed for unforeseen stoppages. That situation is not unlike the present one with this book. Even as the first section was being typeset, contributions came in. Much of the information was invaluable and could be incorporated in the captions to the illustrations. The remainder will not have been lost. It will be deposited in the club archives and will reappear in future issues of *Harlequinade*. No doubt it will be studied carefully when the 150th anniversary comes up in the year 2016.

Inevitably some readers will ask, 'Why didn't X get a mention? He did a lot for the club'. The answer is: 'Did you send in anything about him?'

One of the 'injury time' contributions came from D.R.(Rhys) Williams, a prop forward who joined the club in 1961. His brother, Tudor Williams, played many fine games at full-back when Hiller was not available. As their father was a famous Welsh international, that is hardly surprising. Rhys came in during what might be called 'the last of the good old days', when training was not at its keenest. 'I can recall a turn-out on one occasion which resulted in three-a-side touch Rugby being played and I seem to recall that was not all that uncommon,' he wrote.

However Bob Hiller introduced a sterner regime which encompassed a forty-five-minute 'warm up' before each game. Players found the game distinctly less strenuous than these preliminaries.

Earl Kirton then came on the scene. 'Particularly memorable among Earl's recruiting successes were Chris Barrett, who served the club both on and off the field for many years, and Terry Claxton followed by other members of his family who have played such stalwart roles in the Quins front row for a long period.'

Rhys Williams recalls the invaluable work put in by Frank Cotterill, who not only served voluntarily in the bar but also master-minded the structural improvements on it. He remembers the 'thankless task' performed by John (brother of Grahame) Murray, who was team secretary for the 'A's. When unexpected shortages developed on Friday nights, he would visit pubs in the Earl's Court Road (known as Kangaroo Valley) and 'search out guys who looked as if they were Rugby players, probably being recent arrivals from South Africa, Australia or New Zealand, to make up the numbers. It is surprising how many good players came to the club this way.'

Williams recalls Bob Hiller as 'a truly exceptional Harlequin', not only for the period he played in the Wanderers before attaining international fame but also the many years afterwards when he played for and encouraged the 'A's until he was well over forty.

'On the wings we had several special characters during the Sixties. Harry Eden was one of them but his sight was not his best asset and the saying at the time was that we had to find a ball with a stone in the middle, so even if Harry couldn't see it, he could hear it. John Cox was also a redoubtable wing. Originally on the Stock Exchange, he gave it up to become a picture restorer and is now one of the experts in this field.

'Another winger was John Coker, an Oxford blue, who, apart from being very fast was a devastating tackler. John would close on the centres at the very moment they got the ball, and hit them so hard, usually at waist level, that they would have the stuffing totally knocked out of them and have little further interest in any practical aspects of the game.

'John Coker was also an outstanding boxer, so much so that when he was at Oxford he was not chosen to box against Cambridge as his prospective opponent would not be equal to the occasion. When chosen to box for Sierra Leone in the Olympic Games, he was unable to do so as there were no gloves large enough for his hands.

'John Gibbs (son of J.C.Gibbs) had tremendous skills with a high-stepping run, but was plagued by injuries throughout his career and never achieved the levels he might have done, though playing some spectacular games. Paul Parkin was a very swift runner, running clean and straight.

'Tim Rutter, by contrast, was a jinking runner with a great side-step and I can recall a number of occasions when he would cut through a mass of opposition players, all within apparent tackling distance.

'At outside-half Billy Coutts showed a lot of promise. Bob Read took over in the mid-Sixties, and at the end of the decade, Campbell Hogg, a New Zealander who was a very great character, held the position.

'From a personal point of view, after spending one and a half seasons in the A teams, I established a berth in the Wanderers and then had the opportunity to play quite a lot in the First XV as deputy for either Grahame Murray or David Wrench over the next six or seven years before holding the place on my own for a period at the end of the Sixties. I continued to play a mixture of first-team and Wanderers rugby until about 1972, thereafter Wanderers until 1976, when I captained an 'A' team for another three or four years.'

However, he played his last game when the club was on tour in the USA. The match in Boston took place on a school football ground where a barbecue had been held the previous week. 'As a result, the pitch was in poor condition, and littered with bits of broken material, including glass. Ian Stoppani led a glass-picking exercise which involved everyone present bending down every other pace to pick up some piece of dangerous material. For all the world it looked like a load of hens in a farmyard and quickly was accompanied by the clucking noises associated therewith.'

Much has been said about the match-winning qualities of the Harlequins' back division. However, the final test of strength for any team comes in the front row of the scrum. That is the point in which many of our opponents have tried to dominate by using their 'hard men'. But since the days of 'Holly' Ward they have usually come off the worse in some very bruising encounters. Much of the Harlequins success has been established 'up front' by players like Robin Prescott, Sandy Sanders, David Wrench, Grahame Murray, Terry Claxton and Roger Looker, to name but a few. The tradition continues.

EXTRA-TIME

The Quins' First XV in 1924-5. Howard Marshall is seated extreme left, then Hamilton-Wickes, Stoop, Wakefield, W.G.Davies and W.J.A.Davies.

The First XV in 1932-3. H.J.Gould is standing second left. P.E.Dunkley is the captain. On his left is R.Bolton.

C.G.Stanley (Harlequins) tackles a Northampton player in 1929.

A scene from the Twenties. The Harlequins beat Cambridge University 22-5. No 18's shorts were long, even by the standards of those days.

213

Above: F.W.Simpson (Army) tackles H.C.Pattison (Quins) in 1933. Opposite (top): Harlequins beat Oxford 18-11 in 1937. The Oxford right wing, Prince Obolensky, was closely marked by R.B.Horsley. Opposite (bottom): Whyte gets the ball away against Richmond in 1955.

A match against Rosslyn Park in 1937. Above: Action near the Rosslyn Park goal-line. Opposite: Ken Chapman is outreached. Below: M.E.Golding (Harlequins) passing out.

Action from a scratch game in 1939. Top: Ken Chapman (21) is tackled. Middle: Chapman and R.E.Prescott toss up. Bottom: J.L.Crichton (also wearing 21) converts with Prescott on the ground.

Above: N.A.Steel (Quins) beating London Scottish to the ball in September 1939. Opposite page (top): Harlequins beat St Bartholomew's Hospital 6-3 in this wartime game. Opposite page (bottom): A game against Bath in 1937. The figure at right is W.S.Kemble, after passing.

Flying tackle in an early post-war game in which the Harlequins defeated Cambridge University 22-5.

A match against Richmond at the White City in 1958. K.Pontin, the Quins' scrum-half, is trying to obtain the ball.

The Wanderers in 1950.

Action from the Thirties. A Harlequin forward, trying to force his way through the loose, falls into the hands of D.G.Coles, the Oxford University front-row forward.

The teams for the match to celebrate the 50th anniversary of the first game to be played at Twickenham in 1909. Survivors of the 1909 match, which was played on 2 October

that year against Richmond and in front of a crowd of some two thousand, are pictured in the middle row.

A scene from the Harlequins versus Oxford University match at Twickenham in January 1960. A.H.M.Hoare of the Quins is tackled by an Oxford player. Five months later,

Harlequinade, *the club magazine, was established. The Editor asked for more 'spotters'
to watch 'A' team games so that their members might be considered for the First XV.*

Jeremy Spencer passing out in 1959.

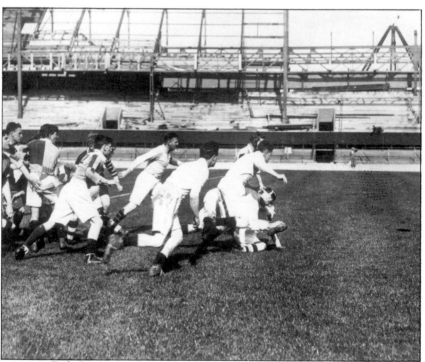

Early days at Twickenham. Play goes on whilst the stand is half-built.

Andy Harriman side-stepping a Rosslyn Park player in 1991. The photograph is by J.McCabe.

Simon Halliday supported by Rob Glenister, in action against Saracens, 1990.

Craig Luxton is presented to Sandy Sanders before the 1990 Middlesex Sevens

Everton Davis in a similar pose at Twickenham.

Now it's Rob Glenister's turn.

The introductions are complete as Adrian Thompson meets Mr Sanders.

The friendly face of Rugby Football. Micky Skinner signs his autograph for two young admirers.

The Harlequins team which won the Wang Invitation Sevens at Richmond in 1989.

Stuart Thresher in full flight against Rosslyn Park in 1991.

The Quins' 1991 Sevens squad, winners of the Middlesex competition.

Harriman is about to throw a long pass during the 1991 Middlesex Sevens.

Everton Davis getting into his stride at Twickenham.

Richard Langhorn wins the ball against Northampton in the 1991 Pilkington Cup Final.

233

PRESIDENTS

1886 .... W.J.COMPTON	1920-1949 .... A.D.STOOP
1887-1890 .... C.JOB	1950-80 .... W.W.WAKEFIELD
1891-1897 .... F.S.WATTS	1981-89 .... K.H.CHAPMAN
1898-1914 .... W.A.SMITH	1990- .... D.K.BROOKS
1915-1919 .... Vacant	

David Brooks, president of the Harlequin FC in 1991.

Harlequins presidents of the Rugby Football Union. Standing (left to right): D.K.Brooks, A.A.Grimsdell, D.L.Sanders. Seated: A.G.Butler, K.H.Chapman, M.R.Steele-Bodger.

A.E.Agar, another former president of the RFU. He brings the total of Quins men who have held this office to eleven, a record from one English club (see page 116).

Harlequins' current chairman Roger Looker, a former England Under-23s international, powerful prop forward and most efficient secretary.

SECRETARIES

1872-74	W.A.SMITH	1920-38	A.D.STOOP
1875	A.F.BASSANO	1939-44	Vacant, World War Two
1876	G.W.PERHAM	1945	A.D.STOOP
1877-85	Vacant	1946-49	K.H.CHAPMAN
1886-87	H.S.JOHNSTONE	1950-59	H.J.GOULD
1888-89	A.EILOART	1960-64	D.A.WHITING
1890-91	H.C.CRUSOE	1965-67	W.WIGGANS
1892-96	H.P.SURTEES	1968-70	P.C.FORBES
1897-99	J.N.HILL	1971	W.WIGGANS
1900-04	R.C.HAYWARD	1972-78	J.SELDON
1905-14	A.D.STOOP	1979-81	R.F.LOOKER
1915-18	Vacant, World War One	1982-91	C.M.HERRIDGE
1919	W.P.WARD		

Harlequins' current secretary, Colin Herridge, a former scrum-half who came to the club via Nottingham and Rosslyn Park. He also served as chairman of the playing committee.

Peter Winterbottom, club captain of the Harlequin FC in 1991.

CAPTAINS

1868-1870	E.E.CLARKE	1930-1931	P.W.ADAMS
1870-1873	E.WALKER	1932	J.C.GIBBS
1874	W.WATSON	1933-1935	P.E.DUNKLEY
1875-1876	G.W.PERHAM	1936-1938	K.H.CHAPMAN
1877	C.E.GRASEMAN	1945	K.H.CHAPMAN
1878	A.TILLYER	1946	B.D.NAPPER
1879	H.WATTS	1947	J.R.C.MATTHEWS
1880-1884	F.W.BURNAND	1948	W.W.JACKSON
1885	A.A.SURTEES	1949-1950	J.R.C.MATTHEWS
1886	G.B.JAMES	1952-1953	D.K.BROOKS
1887	A.B.CIPRIANI	1954-1958	R.M.BARTLETT
1888-1891	A.A.SURTEES	1959-1960	R.W.D.MARQUES
1892-1893	A.B.CIPRIANI	1961	J.S.ABBOTT
1894-1895	S.B.PEECH	1962-1964	C.M.PAYNE
1896	C.M.WELLS	1965-1966	G.C.MURRAY
1897	J.D.WITTAKER	1967	D.F.B.WRENCH
1898-1899	R.F.CUMPERLEDGE	1968-1969	R.B.HILLER
1900	H.O.MILLS	1970-1971	R.H.LLOYD
1901	W.L.FURRELL	1972	E.KIRTON
1902-1905	C.E.L.HAMMOND	1973	M.J.MASON
1906-1914	A.D.STOOP	1974-1976	N.O.MARTIN
1919	N.B.HUDSON	1977-1978	D.A.COOKE
1920	W.W.WAKEFIELD	1979	A.C.ALEXANDER
1921	H.B.T.WAKELAM		T.CLAXTON
1922-1923	V.G.DAVIES	1980	T.CLAXTON
1924	W.W.WAKEFIELD	1981-1982	R.F.BEST
1925	V.G.DAVIES	1983-1987	D.H.COOKE
1926	H.P.MARSHALL	1987-1989	J.OLVER
1927-1929	W.W.WAKEFIELD	1990-	P.J.WINTERBOTTOM

Internationals who have played for The Harlequins

ENGLAND

P J Ackford
A E Agar
T J M Barrington
R M Bartlett
T B Batchelor
I D S Beer
N O Bennett
J G G Birkett
R Bolton
P W P Brook
H Brougham
C J S Butcher
A G Butler
V H Cartwright
W D C Carling
D A Cooke
D H Cooke
G S Conway
J D Currie
T Danby
V G Davies
W J A Davies
W P C Davies
A M Davis
G J Dean
E W Dillon
P J Dixon
P E Dunkley
C K T Faithful
H D Freakes
D J Gay

J C Gibbs
N Gibbs
J E Greenwood
G G Gregory
S J Halliday
E A Hamilton-Hill
R H Hamilton-Wickes
C E L Hammond
V S J Harding
A T Harriman
B C Hartley
R Hiller
M Hofmeyr
E L Horsfall
J C Hubbard
G L Jeffery
H J Kittermaster
N A Labuschagne
H C C Laird
D Lambert
W R M Leake
J Leonard
R H Lloyd
A H MacIlwaine
R W D Marques
V R Marriott
N O Martin
R M Marshall
J R C Matthews
A F Maynard
H Millett

B C Moore
A R Mullins
J Mycock
B E Nicholson
M J Novak
J Olver
S H Osborne
A C Palmer
G V Palmer
C M Payne
D Pears
D G Perry
M S Phillips
I J Pitman
R W Poulton
R E Prescott
H L Price
J S R Reeve
G D Roberts
V G Roberts
W H M Rose
J L B Salmon
D L Sanders
K Savage
J A Schofield
E K Scott
J S M Scott
H J H Sibree
N Silk
M G Skinner
J Spencer

N C Starmer-Smith
J H Steeds
M R Steele-Bodger
C B Stevens
A E Stoddart
A D Stoop
F M Stoop
D H Swayne
J W R Swayne
B H Travers

D B Vaughan
W W Wakefield
A L Warr
R G H Weighill
C M Wells
P Wilkinson
J G Willcox
J E Williams
J M Williams
P N Williams

D S Wilson
P J Winterbottom
C G Woodruff
C R Woodward
A J Wordsworth
J R B Worton
D F B Wrench
J R C Young

W.W.Wakefield playing in the 1928 Middlesex Sevens semi-final against Edgware.

SCOTLAND

G A Birkett
R I Cramb
W Cuthbertson
E A J Fergusson
A L Gracie
M L Grant
J Greenwood
J E Hutton
J J McPartlin
I G Milne
W B Young

IRELAND

C E St John Beamish
W F Browne
W R F Collis
M J Daly
H de Lacy
V J Lyttle
N F McGrath
J R Synge
R J H Uprichard

AUSTRALIA

T Coker

FRANCE

A Verger
G Stener

WALES

F J V Ford
H Mainwaring
R C C Thomas

USA

P Dawkins
W Jefferson

CANADA

M Luke

NEW ZEALAND

N H Allen
B G Fraser
A M Haden
C Hogg
E W Kirton
D S Loveridge
J E Manchester
P J Whiting
S S Wilson

JAPAN

T Fujiwara

FIJI

B Tikousova

ROMANIA

S Luric

Quins' skipper Peter Winterbottom playing for England in 1991.

Harlequins' Will Carling about to score for England.

Paul Ackford in action against Wales.

D.L.Sanders, Harlequins' England international, seen here playing for Major Stanley's XV against Oxford University in 1955. The result was 21-all. 'Sandy' Sanders later became president of the Rugby Football Union.

Micky Skinner, an England international whose long hair would probably have caused Quins of old to wince.

Andy Harriman, formerly of Radley and a Cambridge blue. But for injury he would have won more England honours.

Former England international Bob Hiller, now a vice-president of the Harlequin FC.

SUBSCRIBERS

Presentation Copies
1 The Harlequin Football Club
2 The Rugby Football Union • 3 The Rugby Football Museum

4 Philip Warner
5 D K Brooks
6 R F Looker
7 P Winterbottom
8 George Plumtree
9 Ian Marshall
10 Denys B Gardiner
11 Denys B Gardiner
12 Christopher Boyle
13 John R Folds
14 James B Chadney
15 Wg/Cdr J Seldon OBE
16 T J Titheridge
17 Simon J Cooke
18 David Page
19 J D Bell
20 Michael Frank
    Claxton
21 Michael Frank
    Claxton
22 Chris Uttley
23 Chris Knott
24 John Sharp
25 Frank O'Keefe
26 Noël M K Vinsen
27 Sir David Steel
28 J H Hindmarsh
29 J H Hindmarsh
30 Raymond Marshall
31 Malcolm Horsman
32 G E Loader
33 Paul Edwards
34 Roger Nicholls
35 Walter Hayes CBE
36 David Judd
37 Ian D S Beer
38 Peter Charles Butler

39 Michael J King
40 Gavin John Thompson
41 Peter Smith
42 C J Messer
43 G H Roberts
44 D Bulmer
45 Paul E M Jarrett
46 T D Morgan
47 Mark R Everard
48 R F Crichton
49 Tim Goldring
50 Brian Aungiers
51 Mike Peskin
52 Mike Peskin
53 Mike Peskin
54 Christopher C
    Townsend
55 Geoff Cox
56 P C Jackson
57 Colin I C MacGregor
58 Edward G Rossdale
59 S P J Wadsted
60 M Campbell
61 Reginald Bolton
62 Jonathan C Bolton
63 Geoffrey R John
64 John Moore-Gillon
65 Suzie Moore-Gillon
66 Archie Angus
67 John Cater
68 Ian Rowe
69 John R Southgate
70 John R Southgate
71 John R Southgate
72 G R Walker
73 Roy Croucher
74 V R A Scott-Oldfield

75 Tony Howitt
76 S G H Pattisson
77 Mark Bradley
78 W T Moonie
79 M R Johnson
80 Peter Marson
81 Peter Marson
82 Peter Marson
83 Peter B Richardson
84 Paul D Jackson
85 Paul D Jackson
86 S H Wilcock
87 R W D Marques
88 Brian Schofield
89 W A J Leaver
90 Jesse Charles Victor
    Lyons
91 Peter C Forbes
92 Peter C Forbes
93 Peter C Forbes
94 Peter C Forbes
95 William Petch
96 Dr Richard Rossdale
97 Sir Roy Austen-Smith
98 J C Gibbs
99 Sam Stephen
100 T Bradshaw-
    Isherwood
101 Gerald Stafford
    Hamilton
102 J R Cole
103 W A Moore
104 Stephen R
    Pendlebury
105 George Bartlett QC
106 Robert Luck
107 Philip R Bentham

108 Lord Vaux of Harrowden (John Gilbey)
109 A P Goodman
110 R S Rawle
111 Dr P R Rawle
112 Stephen Pam
113 Simon H Allen
114 Alan Gunner
115 Denzil Gunner
116 Edward Gunner
117 Dr B Manners
118 Mr & Mrs D N C Dumeresque
119 Mr & Mrs D N C Dumeresque
120 G C Tallett
121 John Crouch
122 M A Stary
123 Colin Herridge
124 Richard L Phillips
125 K N Rolls
126 Norman Kearon
127 B C Whitaker
128 T S T Key
129 David Hodges
130 Keith G Jones
131 Mark Raymond Green
132 Peter J Spooner
133 J C Lovatt
134 Edward Morris
135 B E Lambert
136 Mrs C J Blendell
137 Mrs A J Elliott
138 Gary Pettet
139 C S Thomas
140 J B Beldham
141 Charles Abram
142 Charles Abram
143 S R T Penniston
144 Mark Maley
145 Mark Maley
146 Maurice E Kershaw
147 Robert B Storey

148 M J Daly
149 R T H Daly
150 M A F Raw
151 Norman Brunskill
152 Norman Brunskill
153 Norman Brunskill
154 Norman Brunskill
155 John H E Howorth
156 Tristan Brentnall
157 P A Negretti
158 P A Negretti
159 P A Negretti
160 C G Langtree
161 C G Langtree
162 Capt K Edwards
163 Keith J Leslie
164 George Stephens
165 William Stephens
166 Paul Stubbs
167 J M Katz
168 J D Samson
169 Thomas Neville Stephenson (joined 1929)
170 Mike Barrett
171 Gerald Carpenter
172 His Honour Thomas Pigot QC
173 Richard Carr
174 Michael D Gibson
175 W M Jackson
176 S J Wheeler
177 S J Wheeler
178 Bill Ross
179 Gordon W Ralph
180 Munch
181 Munch
182 Munch
183 Malcolm Hoskinson
184 Paul R J Beard
185 Roger Looker
186 Roger Looker
187 Roger Looker
188 B D Napper

189 Daniel J Lloyd
190 Tony Ridge
191 David W Perry
192 W Elton Davies
193 Michael Joseph Edwards
194 R J Snell
195 Christopher Scott North
196 B F Hutchins
197 Phil Davies
198 Ray Harrison
199 C J Scovell
200 Sir Patrick Meaney
201 S G Fowler
202 Nick Silk
203 Paddy J McEvoy
204 David Robb
205 Jon Ortuzar
206 D L Sanders
207 R S P Duckworth
208 Edward G Payne
209 Edward G Payne
210 Adam N G Fox
211 J M R Hagger
212 Tony D Gathercole
213 Tudor Williams
214 J L B Salmon
215 Dr B Hemphill
216 N P O'Brien
217 Peter Doran
218 W R Grimsdell
219 Duncan Wood
220 E J Hudson
221 Nigel Jones
222 Nigel Jones
223 G N T Ferguson
224 C J G Yeldham
225 Keith Standring
226 C R Kelly
227 C R Kelly
228 Russell Thomas
229 Anthony Salmon
230 G C Murray

231 Geoffrey Rutland
232 Richard Brasher
233 George S B Honey DFC
234 Derek A Whiting
235 B S N Band
236 A R Mason
237 H J Moon
238 Julian Easterbrook
239 Paul Bryson Higgins
240 V G Roberts
241 Hugh Forbes
242 Hugh Forbes
243 Russell Dean Turner
244 Russell Dean Turner
245 T A Lewis
246 T A Lewis
247 David Scott Currie
248 John Gronow
249 Martin J B Ledner
250 John D Aitken
251 J J Gardner
252 R J Lawless
253 George Coppen
254 George William Dryden
255 George William Dryden
256 Jonathan W Stocker
257 P K Growdon
258 C O Munton
259 N C G Raffle
260 David Morgan
261 Michael J Harrison
262 Nigel Teasdale
263 Jeremy Swann
264 Thomas Michael Edbrooke
265 Neels Rossouw
266 Geoffrey Archer
267 P J Grant
268 R G Fearn
269 Pat Orr
270 Hugh Saville

271 Rod Abbott
272 Rod Abbott
273 J R Thomas
274 T A Band
275 E B D Waldy
276 R W Thompson
277 P G K Sutton
278 Peter Everard
279 William Vickery Fuller
280 Everton Davis
281 Duncan Harris
282 David Langford
283 Charles W Langford
284 Henry H Pollard
285 Miss Alison Broadbent
286 Gerard Carpenter
287 Bob Read
288 Catherine Arnot
289 Rodney R Osborne
290 G Collier
291 Michael Perry
292 Timothy Atkin
293 Alan D Cooke
294 Debbie Gadd
295 David R Fisher
296 Telfer Saywell
297 D Fry
298 David Puddle
299 Joe Pendock
300 Joe Pendock
301 Simon Wilde
302 M J Collins
303 A W Betournay
304 Robin Wells
305 W S Gibbs
306 Rhys Williams
307 Tudor Williams
308 W David Blenkinsop
309 Graham Cooper
310 Reg Kindred
311 Reg Kindred
312 Mark Samuel Pettit

313 Bob Thomas
314 Stephen Edlmann
315 M R M Evans
316 John Ashwell Couch
317 Donald Kerr
318 Major Peter Stoop
319 Mr Richard Stoop
320 Mr Jason Stoop
321 Philip M Norvill
322 Michael T Wardley
323 Michael T Wardley
324 Kevin D Grindey
325 J P S England
326 Stephen Kimble
327 Alan K Schofield
328 John E M Stevenson
329 David M Stileman
330 Stephen John Hancock
331 C J Cullinane
332 G M Paterson
333 Brian & Shirley Radford
334 Andrew David Radford
335 F A 'Sandy' Hone
336 David Dance
337 Bruce M Warman
338 Andrew Morey
339 Geoff Morey
340 R W G Leeds
341 Ralph Wheeler
342 Ralph Wheeler
343 Mark Bolton
344 Howell Thomas OBE
345 Nicholas & David Wootton
346 Stuart Thomas
347 John Denning
348 P D G Ross
349 Peter 'PJ' Johnston
350 Stuart N Williams
351 D F B Wrench
352 Joanna Rose Blythe

353 Gareth Price
354 Andy Stewart
355 P J Fuller
356 Michael Catherwood
357 Barry Northwood
358 Edward R C Bliss
359 Patrick C R Orr
360 Diallo Jacques
361 Paul Douglas Snare
362 Vincent Walker
363 John Knox
   Montgomerie
364 C M A Sheasby
365 Mr Raymond L
   McCormack
366 David Frederic
   William Bradley
367 Ross Coad
368 Ian M Burrell
369 Malcolm Coombs
370 C J M Ellerington
371 Lt-Col P D F Cleaver
372 Simon Chandler
373 Nicholas Cross
374 Nicholas Cross
375 Nicholas Cross
376 Nicholas Cross
377 Peter H Hind-Fletcher
378 John Brian Birkett
379 Mr Duncan Beardsley
   MA (Oxon)
380 Lt-Col F G G Rapsey
381 Gavin P B Wakley
382 Colin Buckley
383 Jack Maddison
384 E Hoskins Lloyd
   TD HM
385 Sydney Dowse
   MC AEM
386 Bryan L Rodbard
387 Deborah A Rodbard
388 Gerald Postlethwaite
389 Gerald Postlethwaite
390 Gerald Postlethwaite

391 Gerald Postlethwaite
392 A J Hockley
393 J M Hockley
394 G D Hockley
395 David Barclay
396 Mr Robin Plunkett
397 Master Joe Plunkett
398 Ian E Butler
399 William Wiggans
400 Michèle Wiggans
401 Robert Catcher
402 A M Davis
403 Shaun Taylor
404 John Harris
405 John Gibbs
406 A P Challinor
407 Tony Short
408 J H W Butcher
409 John Greenwood
410 Leon Walkden
411 David Michael Snare
412 John Cook
413 M J Mason
414 F M B Killick
415 N J Killick
416 Jeff Butterfield
417 Christopher M
   Horner
418 Miss L Conlan
419 The Ingmire Family
420 John Philip James
421 Donald Bulmer
422 P E Hodge
423 Rupert R M Jones
424 Allan E Parker
425 Wg/Cdr G Strange
   RAF (Ret'd)
426 Neil A Pidduck
427 Bob Hiller
428 Philip Rodney
   Pollard
429 Michael Rodney
   Pollard
430 Valerie Evans

431 Stan Ashbridge
432 R C Rees
433 David A W Watts
434 Gary Claxton
435 Rex Rowe
436 T A Parkhouse
437 Tim Titheridge
438 Mr Sidney D Stevens
439 Lt-Col R A Rodick
   OBE
440 'Chips' Fretwell
441 Philip R Noakes
   OBE
442 Frank Lovis
443 A F Horwell
444 Roger Reid
445 H J R Lane
446 Tim Caffyn
447 Dee Southgate
448 G C Anderson
449 P G Sandford
450 Dr N L Lewis
451 Jack Robertson
   Dow
452 Frank Page
453 Laurence J Lando
454 Simeon J Lando
455 C G Woodruff
456 Geoff Ashby
457 Alan Grimsdell
458 Alan Grimsdell
459 John Edwards
460 Miss C L Berwick
461 Christopher
   Northwood
462 Malcolm Caldwell
463 Joe Glaxton
464 Ian P Carter
465 J R Maries
466 Will Wall
467 K J H Mallett
468 Trevor E Humphreys
469 Clive De B Hovell